FROM
MICHAEL FRAYN

A SEARCH FOR AN UNDERSTANDING OF THE BIG QUESTIONS OF LIFE

MICHAEL
FRAYN
THE
HUMAN
TOUCH

OUR PART IN
THE CREATION OF
A UNIVERSE

ff

GRANTA 95, AUTUMN 2006
www.granta.com

EDITOR   Ian Jack
DEPUTY EDITOR   Matt Weiland
MANAGING EDITOR   Fatema Ahmed
ASSOCIATE EDITOR   Liz Jobey
EDITORIAL ASSISTANT   Helen Gordon

CONTRIBUTING EDITORS   Diana Athill, Simon Gray, Isabel Hilton,
Sophie Harrison, Blake Morrison, John Ryle, Sukhdev Sandhu, Lucretia Stewart

FINANCE   Geoffrey Gordon, Morgan Graver
SALES DIRECTOR   Frances Hollingdale
MARKETING AND SUBSCRIPTIONS   Gill Lambert
IT MANAGER   Mark Williams
TO ADVERTISE CONTACT   Kate Rochester, ksrochester@granta.com
PRODUCTION ASSOCIATE   Sarah Wasley
PROOFS   Lesley Levene

PUBLISHER   Sigrid Rausing

GRANTA PUBLICATIONS, 2-3 Hanover Yard, Noel Road, London N1 8BE
Tel +44 (0)20 7704 9776 Fax +44 (0)20 7704 0474
e-mail for editorial: editorial@granta.com

In the United States, Granta is published in association with Grove/Atlantic Inc,
841 Broadway, 4th Floor, New York, NY 10003

TO SUBSCRIBE go to www.granta.com
or call 020 7704 0470 or e-mail subs@granta.com
A one-year subscription (four issues) costs £27.95 (UK), £35.95 (rest of Europe)
and £42.95 (rest of the world).

Granta is printed and bound in Italy by Legoprint. The paper used in this publication meets the
minimum requirements of American National Standard for Information Sciences—Permanence of
Paper for Printed Library Materials, ANSI Z39.48-1984.

Front cover photograph taken by Albert Smith, 1950
Back cover photograph taken by Howard Sooley, 2006
Design: Slabmedia

ISBN 0-903141-88-4

AUTUMN 06

From the freshest new voices to international prize winners, from the personal to the public and the lyrical to the political — hear the best in writing in all its breadth and brilliance at London's year-round literature festival.

14 Sep	**Qissat** – Short Stories by Palestinian Women
26 Sep	**Mark Haddon**
30 Sep	**William Boyd**
3 Oct	**Martin Amis**
10 Oct	**War and Peace** – New Russian Writing
24 – 29 Oct	**Poetry International** – over thirty of the very best poets from the UK and around the globe in a six-day starburst
22 Nov	**Michael Frayn** with **John Carey** The Human Touch: A Life in Writing
28 Nov	**A.C. Grayling** and **Mark Kurlansky** Fighting Talk: Pacifism, War and International Relations
2 Dec	**Irvine Welsh**
5 Dec	**Sophie Woolley** – When to Run

SHARON OLDS © Catherine Mauger

LUKE WRIGHT

ZENA EDWARDS

WILLIAM BOYD

MARTIN AMIS

IRVINE WELSH

SOPHIE WOOLLEY

Box Office: 08703 800 400   **www.rfh.org.uk/literature**

LOVED ONES

GRANTA

THE ✿ TIMES
Cheltenham
Literature Festival
6-15 October 2006

in association with

OTTAKAR'S

Box Office
01242 227979

Brochure Hotline
01242 237377

www.cheltenhamfestivals.com

CONTRIBUTORS

Chimamanda Ngozi Adichie grew up in Nigeria. She is the author of *Purple Hibiscus* (HarperPerennial/Anchor Books) and, most recently, *Half of a Yellow Sun* (Fourth Estate/Knopf). An extract appeared in *Granta* 92.

Georgia Blain lives in Australia and is the author of four novels. She first appeared in the magazine with 'The Germaine Tape' in *Granta* 70. 'Mao Comes to Sydney' is an extract from her forthcoming book of personal essays: *Births, Deaths, Marriages*.

Claire Keegan was raised on a farm in County Wicklow, Ireland. Her short-story collection, *Antarctica*, is published by Faber & Faber in the UK and by Grove/Atlantic in the US where it was a *Los Angeles Times* Book of the Year. Her stories have won the William Trevor Prize and the Olive Cook Award. Her new collection, *Walk the Blue Fields*, will be published by Faber in spring 2007. She lives in rural Ireland.

John Lanchester's 'Early Retirement' is taken from his memoir, *Family Romance*, to be published in the spring by Faber & Faber in the UK and by Putnam's in the US. He is the author of three novels, most recently *Fragrant Harbour* (Faber & Faber/Penguin).

James Lasdun was the winner of this year's inaugural National Short Story Competition. He has published several books of poetry and fiction, most recently a novel, *Seven Lies* (Jonathan Cape/W. W. Norton). An extract appeared in *Granta* 89.

Melanie McFadyean is a freelance journalist, contributing regularly to the London *Guardian*. She teaches journalism at City University, London.

David Malouf was born in Brisbane, Australia. His novels include *The Conversations at Curlow Creek* and *Remembering Babylon* (Vintage), which won the IMPAC Prize in 1996. In 2000 his libretto for an opera based on *Jane Eyre* received its world premiere. 'Every Move You Make' is the title story from his new collection which will be published by Chatto & Windus in January 2007. His short story 'Closer' appeared in *Granta* 68.

Rebecca Miller's novel, *The Private Lives of Pippa Lee*, will be published by Farrar Straus & Giroux in the US in 2008. Her collection of short stories, *Personal Velocity*, is published by Black Swan in the UK and by Grove Press in the US. 'Mrs Covet' was commissioned by RTE radio in Ireland and read aloud by Julianne Moore.

Jeremy Seabrook's most recent book is *Consuming Cultures: Globilization and Local Lives* (New Internationalist). He contributes to *The Statesman* in Kolkata, *Third World Resurgence* in Malaysia and the London *Guardian*. He is writing a book about English provincial life which is forthcoming from Granta Books. He last appeared in the magazine with 'The End of the Provinces' in *Granta* 90.

Jim Shepard lives in Williamstown, Massachusetts. He is the author of a collection of short stories, *Love and Hydrogen* (Vintage), and five novels, most recently *Project X* (Vintage). His new collection, *Like You'd Understand Anyway*, will be published by Knopf in 2007.

Graham Smith's photographs are in many public and private collections. An earlier photographic essay was published in *Granta* 25. Four of Albert Smith's photographs were bought and exhibited by the Victoria & Albert Musuem, London, and also exhibited at the Tate Gallery, Liverpool.

Jonathan Taylor is a lecturer in English at Loughborough University. His short stories have been published in various magazines and his radio dramas broadcast on various stations. He also runs his own arts organization, Crystal Clear Creators. 'Help, Help, Help' is taken from his memoir, *Take Me Home*, to be published by Granta Books in 2007.

Fan Wu was born in 1973. She grew up on a farm in southern China, where her parents were exiled during the Cultural Revolution. She moved to the United States in 1997 to study at Stanford University. Her first novel, *February Flower*, is published by Picador Asia and will be published in the UK by Picador in spring 2007. She writes in both English and Chinese and is working on a second novel and a short-story collection. She lives in northern California where she works as Web editor.

ESSENTIAL YEARBOOKS

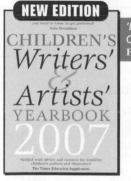
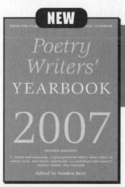

International Literary Festivals 2006/2007

Hanan al-Shaykh
Germaine Greer
Sir VS Naipaul
Martin Amis
Vikram Seth
William Dalrymple
Michael Portillo
Baroness Emma Nicholson
Blake Morrison
Patrick French
Robert Irwin
... the list continues

A celebration of British and Arab arts, cultural and media relations in the Middle East

The Majestic Petra Festival

www.majesticpetra.com
1-3 December, Petra, Jordan
2006

Kitab Festival

The second British-Indian/International Literary and Media Festival to be held in India.
www.kitabfest.org
23-26 February 2007

Next ventures: Istanbul, St Petersburg and Marrakech

For further information and any enquires, please contact
Pablo Ganguli at Pablo.Ganguli@gmail.com

INTRODUCTION

One of the world's unfair divisions is that between the writer and the written-about, and this is nowhere more true than in the literary form called the memoir. Memoirs are very rarely 'about' the person who writes them; among the striking exceptions might be J. R. Ackerley and Diana Athill. Self-depiction is a difficult art if the result is to be both honest and interesting, and more than a list of achievement. To succeed, memoirs usually latch on to the easier and more fruitful business of describing people other than the self, with the memoirist as a witness rather than an actor. In V. S. Pritchett's *A Cab at the Door* it's Pritchett's father we remember—the rackety, philandering Christian Scientist—rather than young Pritchett himself. The same could be said of Blake Morrison's *And When Did You Last See Your Father?* and many other good modern memoirs. Memoirists need lively human subjects outside themselves, and, to be frank, it helps if the subject is dead. The fact of their death often prompts the original impulse to write—to memorialize and to share and illuminate the intimate with a wider audience whose lives are filled with similar intimacies, a good reason to write a book. But it's also true that the dead are handy because you can't offend them and they won't answer back. Silent in their graves, they encourage freedom among the writing classes six feet above.

This is what I mean by 'unfair division'. They have no right of reply. There they are stuck with the only public version of themselves, to be remembered eventually only because of a book (which may be better—or not—than being forgotten by everyone). Once a colleague at *Granta* suggested a good issue might be called 'Dead Parents Hit Back', but of course the difficulty of commissioning the pieces made it impossible to organize. And even if it had been possible—if the dead had been awoken by the fees and energies of the literary agent Andrew Wylie—I think most would have been reluctant to dish the dirt on their writer progeny. Parenthood doesn't bring out the candid best in a writer, which may be connected to the parental ideal of unconditional love for one's children. Is there a good memoir of a child by a parent? Perhaps so, but I haven't read it. Victorians sometimes mourned the premature death of their children in non-fiction. In the present age only fiction (for example, Lionel Shriver's *We Need to Talk about Kevin*) seems able to explore any feeling other than pride and love. This may speak well of us as parents, but it confines memoir to one-way traffic.

'With autobiography there's always another text, a countertext, if you will, to the one presented,' writes Philip Roth's alter ego Zuckerman in *The Facts*, adding, 'It's probably the most manipulative of all literary forms.' *The Facts* is an overlooked book by Roth (in Britain it's hard to find), but it contains priceless wisdom for both the memoir-writer and -reader; 'life-writing' classes should teach it. The book is divided into three parts. In the first part, Roth tells his fictional creation Zuckerman that he is going to take a break from fictionalizing his life and instead write 'the facts'. In the second part, he describes his early life, his women, his troubles, and his first literary success. In the third part, Zuckerman (Roth, of course) takes 'the facts' apart and advises him against publication.

'What you choose to tell in fiction,' writes Zuckerman, 'is different to what you're permitted to tell when nothing's being fictionalized, and in this book you are not permitted to tell what it is you tell best: kind, discreet, careful—changing people's names because you're worried about hurting their feelings—no, this isn't you at your most interesting... You try to pass off here as frankness what looks to me like the dance of the seven veils—what's on the page is like a code for something missing.' And later: 'Even if it's only one per cent that you've edited out, that's the one per cent that counts—the one per cent that's saved for your imagination and that changes everything.'

This issue of *Granta* being called 'Loved Ones', it naturally contains several pieces of memoir. I think they're as honest—sometimes uncomfortably so—as any personal non-fiction can be. But one should always remember Roth's 'countertexts', of which the world is so invisibly full.

A striking difference between British and American literary fiction, at least among its younger writers, is the number of people who need to be thanked. Victorian writers rarely thanked anyone at all in the pages of their books. Who does George Eliot thank for *Middlemarch*? Nobody. An older generation still with us—Roth, for example—will make do with a brief and mysterious dedication: 'To H. J.' For some time now, others have more explicitly mentioned their husbands, or more usually wives, sometimes referring to their 'patience' and 'understanding' and implying how essential both were when the suicidal writer came down from his study and said it was all over and all rubbish, he would never write another word. In the new century among new writers, such brevity would be considered miserly ingratitude. As a judge of *Granta*'s Best of Young American Novelists I've been reading a lot of fiction, short-story collections as well as novels, by writers under thirty-five years old. I can't say what I think of the books themselves—the judging isn't over—but I can say that never before have I read such long acknowledgements in works of fiction.

In the book in front of me now they run to four pages. To get to the end of them is like standing impatiently through the final credits in a cinema until the words 'second-grip' and 'Westrex' appear on the screen. On the first page, the writer thanks and lists 'the good folks' and 'esteemed fellow workshoppers and friends' of his second creative writing school. On the second page, he does the same for his first writing school, plus a few other teachers he's met along the way (one of whom he stuck to 'barnaclelike'). By the third page we've got on to his previous employer and fellow former employees, his agent, his editor, someone called Stacy at Caribou Coffee, and, well, just a bunch of wonderful friends. The fourth page is given over to his mother, his sister, his late wife, his present partner: 'four extraordinary women, all of whom I love without measure'. The only item missing is a grant from the Guggenheim Foundation.

These pages appear at the end of seven short stories, some of which I liked very much. The question is: did all this thanksgiving make me think less of the writer (and therefore, unfairly, less of the stories), and if so why? Certainly, it shouldn't do. To acknowledge the idea that writers and writing need all kinds of sustenance and encouragement, from loving sisters to Stacy with her large lattes down at the Caribou, is gracious behaviour. To thank one's fellow workshoppers and tutors shows that writing can be a very cooperative process, which may be a truer way of looking at it than the caricature of the lonely, struggling genius, as well as a rare and welcome thing in a society obsessed with individual competition. But these generous instincts can also be read less generously. Stories aren't obviously cooperative ventures like plays or films, but perhaps this book really has been produced in a kind of factory, a 'workshop' filled with the sound of relentless verbal carpentry, of sentence-honing and character-shaping, until the hooter sounds and everyone finds an agent or goes home. Perhaps it was one of the dozens of the thanked, 'Donna' or 'Kelly', who produced the phrase 'complicated terrain of the yard' on page thirty-two. Maybe 'Joshua' added the word 'and' to that wonky dialogue on forty-six. There's no reason a good book can't be produced that way, but do we need to know it? It only serves to remind us of the underlying effort, the pain given for our pleasure. Above all, why should the writer imagine we care about any of them? Might it be (and this is the most ungenerous thought of all) that he is mighty pleased with himself—that he thinks his work is so brilliant that its worth needs some explanation?

So far, writers in Britain (and elsewhere) are less given to lengthy acknowledgements, but that may be changing with the steadily increasing number of writing schools at British universities. The book may be at its heart still a solitary act of creation, but the process of learning to write one has become socialized—you might even say industrialized—to the point where Donna, Kelly, Joshua, etc. have indeed earned their mention as the second-grip.

The judges of *Granta*'s Best of Young American Novelists campaign hold their final meeting in New York in October. They are, myself apart: Edmund White and A. M. Homes, novelists and memoirists; Paul Yamazaki of the City Lights bookshop in San Francisco; Meghan O'Rourke, poet and literary editor of *Slate*; and Sigrid Rausing, *Granta*'s publisher. As in the first Best of Young Americans in 1996, our task is to choose twenty writers (from around 150 submitted) who in our view have achieved most or who promise most. New work from the twenty will comprise a special edition of *Granta* to be published next spring.

As it happens, I hope my fellow judges will like the short stories of the anonymous writer above as much as I do, and that they'll ignore the extra-literary question of the acknowledgements. ☐

EVERY MOVE
YOU MAKE
David Malouf

When Jo first came to Sydney, the name she heard in every house she went into was Mitchell Maze. 'This is a Mitchell Maze house,' someone would announce, 'can't you just tell?' and everyone would laugh. After a while she knew what the joke was and did not have to be told. 'Don't tell me,' she'd say, taking in the raw uprights and bare window frames, 'Mitchell Maze,' and her hostess would reply, 'Oh, do you know Mitch? Isn't he the limit?'

They were beach houses, even when they were tucked away in a cul-de-sac behind the Paddington Post Office or into a gully below an escarpment at Castlecrag. The group they appealed to, looking back affectionately to the hidey-holes and tree houses of their childhood, made up a kind of clan. Of artists mostly, painters, session musicians, film-makers, writers for the *National Times* and the *Fin Review*, who paid provisional tax and had kids at the International Grammar School, or they were lawyers at Freehills or Allen, Allen & Hemsley, or investment bankers with smooth manners and bold ties who still played touch rugby at the weekends or belonged to a surf club. Their partners—they were sometimes married, mostly not—worked as arts administrators, or were in local government. A Mitchell Maze house was a sign that you had arrived but were not quite settled.

Airy improvisations, or—according to how you saw it—calculated and beautiful wrecks, a lot of their timber was driftwood blanched and polished by the tide, or had been scrounged from building sites or picked up cheap at demolitions. It had knotholes, the size sometimes of a twenty-cent piece, and was so carelessly stripped that layers of old paint were visible in the grain that you could pick out with a fingernail, in half-forgotten colours from another era: apple green, ox blood, baby blue. A Mitchell Maze house was a reference back to a more relaxed and open-ended decade, an assurance (a reassurance in some cases) that your involvement with the Boom, and all that went with it, was opportunistic, uncommitted, tongue-in-cheek. You had maintained the rage, still had a Che or Hendrix poster tacked to a wall of the garage and kept a fridge full of tinnies, though you *had* moved on from the flagon red. As for Mitch himself, he came with the house. 'Only not often enough,' as one of his clients quipped.

He might turn up one morning just at breakfast time with a claw hammer and rule at the back of his shorts and a load of timber on his shoulder. One of the kids would already have sighted his ute.

'Oh, great,' the woman at the kitchen bench would say, keeping her voice low-keyed but not entirely free of irony. 'Does this mean we're going to get that wall? Hey, kids, here's Mitch. Here's our wall.'

'Hi,' the kids yelled, crowding round him. 'Hi, Mitch. Is it true? Is that why you're here? Are you goin' t'give us a *wall*?'

They liked Mitch, they loved him. So did their mother. But she also liked the idea of a wall.

He would accept a mug of coffee, but when invited to sit and have breakfast with them would demur. 'No, no thanks,' he'd tell them. 'Gotta get started. I'll just drink this while I work.'

He would be around then for a day or two, hammering away till it was dusk and the rosellas were tearing at the trees beyond the deck and dinner was ready; staying on for a plate of pasta and some good late-night talk, then bedding down after midnight in a bunk in the kids' room, 'to get an early start', or, if they were easy about such things, crawling in with a few murmured apologies beside his hosts. Then in the morning he would be gone again, and no amount of calling, no number of messages left at this place or that, would get him back.

Visitors observing an open wall would say humorously, 'Ah, Mitch went off to get a packet of nails, I see.'

Sensitive fellows, quick to catch the sharpening of their partners' voice as it approached the subject of a stack of timber on the living-room floor, or a bathroom window that after eleven months was still without glass, would spring to the alert.

As often as not, the first indication that some provisional but to this point enduring arrangement was about to be renegotiated would be a flanking attack on the house. 'Right, *mate*,' was the message, 'let's get serious here. What about that wall?'

Those who were present to hear it, living as they did in structures no less flimsy than the one that was beginning to break up all around them, would feel a chill wind at their ear.

All this Jo had observed, with amusement and a growing curiosity, for several months before she found herself face to face with the master builder himself.

Jo was thirty-four and from the country, though no one would have called her a country girl. Before that she was from Hungary. Very animated and passionately involved in everything she did, very intolerant of those who did not, as she saw it, demand enough of life, she was a publisher's editor, ambitious or pushy according to how you took these things, and successful enough to have detractors. She herself wanted it all—everything. And more.

'You want too much,' her friends told her. 'You can't have it, you just can't. Nobody can.'

'You just watch me,' Jo told them in reply.

She had had two serious affairs since coming to Sydney, both briefer than she would have wished. She was too intense, that's what her friends told her. The average bloke, the average *Australian* bloke—oh, here it comes, *that* again, she thought—was uncomfortable with dramatics. Intimidated. Put off.

'I don't want someone who's average,' she insisted. 'Even an average Australian.'

She wanted a love that would be overwhelming, that would make a wind-blown leaf of her, a runaway wheel. She was quite prepared to suffer, if that was to be part of it. She would walk barefoot through the streets and howl if that's what love brought her to.

Her friends wrinkled their brows at these stagey extravagances. 'Honestly! Jo!' Behind her back they patronized and pitied her.

In fact they too, some of them, had felt like this at one time or another. At the beginning. But had learned to hide their disappointment behind a show of hard-boiled mateyness. They knew the rules. Jo had not been around long enough for that. She had no sense of proportion. Did she even *know* that there were rules?

They met at last. At a party at Palm Beach, the usual informal Sunday-afternoon affair. She knew as soon as he walked in who it must be. He was wearing khaki shorts, work boots, nothing fancy. An open-necked unironed shirt.

Drifting easily from group to group, noisily greeted with cries and little affectionate pecks on the cheek by the women, and with equally affectionate gestures from the men—a clasp of the shoulder, a hand laid for a moment on his arm—he unsettled the room, that's what she thought, refocused its energies, though she accepted later that the unsettlement may only have been in herself. Through it all he struck her as being remote, untouchable, self-enclosed, though not at all self-regarding. Was it simply that he was shy? When he found her at last she had the advantage of knowing more about him, from the tales she had been regaled with, the houses she had been in, than he could have guessed.

What she was not prepared for was his extraordinary charm. Not his talk—there was hardly any of that. His charm was physical. It had to do with the sun-bleached, salt-bleached mess of his hair and the way he kept ploughing a rough hand through it; the grin that left deep lines in his cheeks; the intense presence, of which he himself seemed dismissive or unaware. He smelled of physical work, but also, she thought, of wood shavings—blond transparent curlings off the edge of a plane. Except that the special feature of his appeal was the rough rather than the smooth.

They went home together. To his place, to what he called 'The Shack', a house on stilts, floating high above a jungle of tree ferns, morning glory and red-clawed coral trees in a cove at Balmoral. Stepping into it, she felt she had been there already. Here at last was the original of all those open-ended, unfinished structures she had been in and out of for the past eight months. When she opened the door to the loo, she laughed. There was no glass in the window. Only a warmish square of night filled with ecstatic insect cries.

She was prepared for the raw, splintery side of him. The sun-cracked lips, the blonded hair that covered his forearms and the darker hair that came almost to his Adam's apple, the sandpapery hands with their scabs and festering nicks. What she could not have guessed at was the whiteness and almost feminine silkiness of his hidden parts. Or the old-fashioned delicacy with which he turned away every attempt on her part to pay tribute to them. It was so at odds with the libertarian mode she had got used to down here.

He took what he needed in a frank, uncomplicated way; was forceful but considerate—all this in appreciation of her own attractions. She was flattered, moved, and in the end felt a small glow of triumph at having so much pleased him. For a moment he entirely yielded, and she felt, in his sudden cry, and in the completeness afterwards with which he sank into her arms, that she had been allowed into a place that in every other circumstance he kept guarded, closed off.

She herself was dazzled. By a quality in him—*beauty* is what she said to herself—that took her breath away, a radiance that burned her lips, her fingertips, every point where their bodies made contact. But when she tried to express this—to touch him as he had touched her and reveal to him this vision she had of him—he resisted. What she felt in his almost angry shyness was a kind of distaste. She retreated, hurt, but was resentful too. It was unfair of him to exert so powerful an appeal and then turn maidenly when he got a response.

She should have seen then what cross-purposes they would be at, and not only in this matter of intimacy. But he recognized her hurt, and in a way, she would discover, that was typical of him, tried out of embarrassment to make amends.

He was sitting up with his back against the bedhead enjoying a smoke. Their eyes met, he grinned; a kind of ease was re-established between them. She was moved by how knocked about he was, the hard use to which he had put his body, the scraps and scrapes he had been through. Her fingertips went to a scar, a deep nick in his cheekbone under the left eye. She did not ask. Her touch was itself a question.

'Fight with an arc lamp,' he told her. His voice had a humorous edge. 'I lost. Souvenir of my brief career as a movie star.'

She looked at him. The grin he wore was light, self-deprecatory. He was offering her one of the few facts about himself—from his childhood, his youth—that she would ever hear. She would learn only later how useless it was to question him on such matters. You got nowhere by asking. If he did let something drop it was to distract you, while some larger situation that he did not want to develop slipped quietly away. But that was not the case on this occasion. They barely knew one another. He wanted, in all innocence, to offer her something of himself.

When he was thirteen—this is what he told her—he had been taken by his mother to an audition. More than a thousand kids had turned up. He didn't want the part, he thought it was silly, but he had got it anyway and for a minute back there, because of that one appearance, had been a household name, a star.

She had removed her hand and was staring.

'What?' he said, the grin fading. He gave her an uncomfortable look and leaned across to the night table to stub out his cigarette.

'I can't believe it,' she was saying. 'I can't believe this. I know who you are. You're Skip Daley!'

'No, I'm not,' he said, and laughed. 'Don't be silly.'

He was alarmed at the way she had taken it. He had offered it as a kind of joke. One of the *least* important things he could have told her.

'But I saw that film! I saw it five times!'

'Don't,' he said. 'It was nothing. I shouldn't have let on.'

But he could have no idea what it had meant to her. What *he* had meant to her.

Newly arrived in the country, a gangly ten year old, and hating everything about this place she had never wanted to come to—the parched backyards, the gravel playground under the pepper trees at her bare public school, the sing-song voices that mocked her accent and deliberately, comically got her name wrong—she had gone one Saturday afternoon to the local pictures and found herself tearfully defeated. In love. Not just with the hard-heeled freckle-faced boy up on the screen, with his round-headed, blond pudding-bowl haircut and cheeky smile, his fierce sense of honour, the odd mixture in him of roughness and shy, broad-vowelled charm, but with the whole barefoot world he moved in, his dog Blue, his hard-bitten parents who were in danger of losing their land, the one-storeyed sun-struck weatherboard they lived in, which was, in fact, just like her own.

More than a place, it was a world of feeling she had broken through to, and it could be hers now because *he* lived in it. She had given up her resistance.

On that hot Saturday afternoon, in that darkened picture theatre in Albury, her heart had melted. Australia had claimed and conquered her. She was shocked and the shock was physical. She had had no idea till then what beauty could do to you, the deep tears it could draw up; how it could take hold of you in the middle of the path and turn you round, fatefully, and set you in a new direction. That was what he could know nothing of.

All that time ago, he had changed her life. And here he was more than twenty years later, in the flesh, looking sideways at her in this unmade lump of a bed.

'Hey,' he was saying, and he put his hand out to lift aside a strand of her hair.

'I just can't get over it,' she said.

'Hey,' he said again. 'Don't be silly! It was nothing. Something my mother got me into. It was all made up. That stupid kid wasn't me. I was a randy little bugger if you want to know. All I could think about was my dick—' and he laughed. 'They didn't show any of that. Truth is, I didn't like myself much in those days. I was too unhappy.'

But he was only getting himself in deeper. Unhappy? He caught the look in her eyes, and to save the situation leaned forward and covered her mouth with his own.

From the start he famished her. It was not in her nature to pause at thresholds but there were bounds she could not cross and he was gently, firmly insistent. He did give himself, but when she too aggressively took the initiative, or crossed the line of what he thought of as a proper modesty, he would quietly turn away. What he was abashed by, she saw, was just what most consumed her, his beauty. He had done everything he could to abolish it. All those nicks and scars. The broken tooth he took no trouble to have fixed. The exposure to whatever would burn or coarsen.

A series of 'spills' had left him, at one time or another, with a fractured collarbone, three bouts of concussion, a broken leg. These punishing assaults on himself were attempts to wipe out an affliction. But all they had done was refine it: bring out the metallic blue of his eyes, show up under the skin, with its network of cracks, the poignancy—that is how she saw it—of his bones.

Leaving him sprawled, that first morning, she had stepped out into the open living room.

Very aware that she was as yet only a casual visitor to his world, and careful of intruding, she picked her way between plates piled with old food and set on tabletops or pushed halfway under chairs, coffee mugs, beer cans, gym socks, ashtrays piled with butts, magazines, newspapers, unopened letters, shirts dropped just anywhere or tossed carelessly over the backs of chairs. A dead light bulb on a glass coffee table rolled in the breeze.

She sat a moment on the edge of a lounger and thought she could hear the tinkling that came from the closed globe, a distant sound, magical and small, but magnified, like everything this morning. The room was itself all glass and light. It hung in mid-air. Neither inside nor out, it opened straight into the branches of a coral tree, all scarlet claws.

She went to the kitchen bench at the window. The sink was piled with coffee mugs and more dishes. She felt free to deal with those, and was still at the sink, watching a pair of rainbow lorikeets on the deck beyond, all his dinner plates gleaming in the rack, when he stepped up behind her in a pair of sagging jockey shorts, still half asleep, rubbing his skull. He kissed her in a light, familiar way. Barely noticing the cleared sink—that was a *good* sign—he ran a glass of water and drank it off, his Adam's apple bobbing. Then kissed her again, grinned and went out on to the deck.

The lorikeets flew off, but belonged here, and soon ventured back.

O ver the weeks, as she came to spend more time there, she began to impose her own sort of order on the place. He did not object. He sat about reading the papers while she worked around him.

The drawers of the desk where he sometimes sat in the evening, wearing reading glasses while he did the accounts, were stuffed with papers—letters, cuttings, prospectuses. There were more papers pushed into cardboard boxes, in cupboards, stacked in corners, piled under beds.

'Do you want to keep any of this?' she would enquire from time to time, holding up a fistful of mail.

He barely looked. 'No. Whatever it is. Just chuck it.'

'You sure?'

'Why? What is it?'

'Letters.'

'Sure. Chuck 'em out.'

'What about these?'

'What are they?'

'Invoices. 1984.'

'No. Just pile 'em up, I'll make a bonfire. Tomorrow maybe.'

S he had a strong need for fantasy, she liked to make things interesting. In their early days together, she took to leaving little love notes for him. Once under the tea caddy, where he would come across it when he went out in the morning, just after six, to make their tea. On other occasions, beside his shaving gear in the bathroom, in one of the pockets of his windcheater, in his work shorts. If he read them he did not mention the fact. It was ages before he told her, in a quarrel, how much these love notes embarrassed him. She flushed scarlet, did not make that mistake again.

He had no sense of fantasy himself. He wasn't insensitive—she was often touched by his thoughtfulness and by the small things he noticed—but he was very straight-up-and-down, no frills. Once, when his film was showing, she asked if they could go and see it. 'What for?' he asked, genuinely surprised. 'It's crap. Anyway, I'd rather forget all that. It wasn't a good time, that. Not for me it wasn't.'

'Because you were unhappy?' she said. 'You told me that, remember?'

But he shut off then, and the matter dropped.

He told her nothing about his past. Nothing significant. And if she asked, he shied away.

'I don't want to talk about it,' was all he'd say. 'I try to forget about what's gone and done with. That's where we're different. You go on and on about it.'

No, I don't, she wanted to argue. You're the one who's hung up on the past. That's why you won't talk about it. What I'm interested in is the present. But all of it. All the little incidental happenings that got you here, that got *us* here, made us the way we are. Seeing that she was still not satisfied, he drew her to him, almost violently—offering her that, his hard presence—and sighed, she did not know for what.

He had no decent clothes that she could discover. Shirts, shorts, jeans—workclothes, not much else. A single tie that he struggled into when he had an engagement that was 'official'. She tried to rectify this. But when he saw the pile of new things on the bed he looked uncomfortable. He took up a blue poplin shirt, fingered it, frowned, put it down.

'I wish you wouldn't,' he said. 'Buy me things. Shirts and that.' He was trying not to seem ungracious, she saw, but was not happy. 'I don't need shirts.'

'But you do,' she protested. 'Look at the one you've got on.'

He glanced down. 'What's wrong with it?'

'It's in rags.'

'Does me,' he said, looking put out.

'So. Will you wear these things or what?'

'I'll wear them,' he said. 'They're bought now. But I don't want you to do it, that's all. I don't *need* things.'

He refused to meet her eye. Something more was being said, she thought. I don't deserve them—was that what he meant? In a sudden rush of feeling for something in him that touched her but which she could not quite catch, she clasped him to her. He relaxed, responded.

'No more shirts, then,' she promised.

'I just don't want you to waste your money,' he said childishly. 'I've got loads of stuff already.'

'I know,' she said. 'You should send the lot of it to the Salvos. Then you'd have nothing at all. You'd be naked, and wouldn't be able to go out, and I'd have you all to myself.' She had, by now, moved in.

'Is that what you want?' he asked, picking up on her lightness, allowing her, without resistance for once, to undo the buttons on the offending shirt.

'You know I do,' she told him.

'Well then,' he said.

'Well then what?'

'Well, you've *got* me,' he said, 'haven't you?'

He had a ukulele. Occasionally he took it down from the top shelf of the wardrobe and, sitting with a bare foot laid over his thigh, played—not happily, she thought—the same plain little tune.

She got to recognize the mood in which he would need to seek out this instrument that seemed so absurdly small in his hands and for which he had no talent, and kept her distance. The darkness in him frightened her. It seemed so far from anything she knew of his other nature.

Some things she discovered only by accident. 'Who's Bobby Kohler?' she asked once, having several times now come across the name on letters.

'Oh, that's me,' he said. '*Was* me.'

'What do you mean?'

'It's my name. My real name. Mitchell Maze is just the name I work under.'

'You mean you changed it?'

'Not really. Some people still call me Bobby.'

'Who does?'

'My mother. A few others.'

'Is it German?'

'Was once, I suppose. Away back. Grandparents.'

She was astonished, wanted to ask more, but could see that the subject was now done with. She might ask but he would not answer.

There were times when he did tell her things. Casually, almost dismissively, off the top of his head. He told her how badly, at sixteen, he had wanted to be a long-distance runner, and shine. How for a whole year he had got up in the dark, before his paper run, and gone out in the growing light to train on the oval at their local showground at Castle Hill. He laughed, inviting her to smile at some picture he could see of his younger self, lean, intense, driven, straining painfully day after day towards a goal he would never reach. She was touched by this. But he was not looking for pity. It was the folly of the thing he was intent on. It appealed to a spirit of savage irony in him that she could not share.

There were no evocative details. Just the bare, bitter facts. He could see the rest too clearly in his mind's eye to reproduce it for hers. She had to do that out of her own experience: Albury. The early-morning frost on the grass. Magpies carolling around a couple of milk cans in the long grass by the road. But she needed more, to fix in a clarifying image the tenderness she felt for him, the sixteen-year-old Bobby Kohler, barefooted, in sweater and shorts, already five inches taller than the Skip Daley she had known, driving himself hard through those solitary circuits of the oval as the sunlight came and the world turned golden around him.

One day she drove out in her lunch hour to see the place. Sat in her car in the heat and dazzle. Walked to the oval fence and took in the smell of dryness. There was less, in fact, than she imagined.

But a week later she went back. His mother lived there. She found the address, and after driving round the suburb for a bit, sat in her car under a paperbark on the other side of the street. Seeing no one in the little front yard, she got out, crossed, climbed the two front steps to the veranda, and knocked.

There was no reply.

She walked to the end of the veranda, which was unpainted, its timber rotting, and peered round the side. No sign of anyone.

Round the back, there was a water tank, painted the usual red, and some cages that might once have held rabbits. She peeped in through the window on a clean little kitchen with a religious calendar—was he a Catholic? He'd never told her that—and into two bedrooms on either side of a hall, one of which, at one time, must have been his.

He lived here, she told herself. For nearly twenty years. Something must be left of him.

She went down into the yard and turned the bronze key of the tap, lifting to her mouth a cupped handful of the cooling water. She felt like a ghost returning to a world that was not her own, nostalgic for what she had never known; for what might strike her senses strongly enough—the taste of tank water, the peppery smell of geraniums—to bring back some immediate physical memory of the flesh. But that was crazy. What was she doing? She had *him*, didn't she?

That night, touching the slight furriness, in the dark, of his earlobe, smelling the raw presence of him, she gave a sob and he paused in his slow lovemaking.

'What is it?' he said. 'What's the matter?'

She shook her head, felt a kind of shame—what could she tell him? That she'd been nosing round a backyard in Castle Hill looking for some ghost of him? He'd think she was mad.

'Tell me,' he said.

His face was in her hair. There was a kind of desperation in him. But this time she was the one who would not tell.

He was easy to get on with and he was not. They did most things together; people thought of them as a couple, they were happy. He came and went without explanation, and she learned quickly enough that she either accepted him on these terms or she could not have him at all. Without quite trying to, he attracted people, and when 'situations' developed was too lazy, or too easy-going, to extract himself. She learned not to ask where he had been or what he was up to. That wasn't what made things difficult between them.

She liked to have things out. He wouldn't allow it. When she raged he looked embarrassed. He told her she was over-dramatic, though the truth was that he liked her best when she was in a passion, it was the very quality in her that had first attracted him. What he didn't like were scenes. If she tried to make a scene, as he called it, he walked out.

'It's no use shouting at one another,' he'd tell her, though in fact he never shouted. 'We'll talk about it later.' Which meant they wouldn't talk at all.

'But I *need* to shout,' she shouted after him.

Later, coming back, he would give a quick sideways glance to see if she had 'calmed down'.

She hadn't usually. She'd have made up her mind, after a bout of tears, to end things.

'What about a cuppa?' he'd suggest.

'What you won't accept—' she'd begin.

'Don't,' he'd tell her. 'I've forgotten all about it.' As if the hurt had been his. Then, 'I'm sorry. I don't want you to be unhappy.'

'I'm not,' she'd say. 'Just—exasperated.'

'Oh, well,' he'd say. 'That's all right then.'

What tormented her was the certainty she felt of his nursing some secret—a lost love perhaps, an old grief—that he could not share. Which was there in the distance he moved into; there in the room, in the bed beside her; and might, she thought, have the shape on occasion of that ukulele tune, and which she came to feel as a second presence between them.

It was this distance in him that others were drawn to. She saw that clearly now. A horizon in him that you believed you alone could reach. You couldn't. Maybe no one could. After a time it put most people off; they cut their losses and let him go. But that was not her way. If she let him go, it would destroy her. She knew that because she knew herself.

There was a gleam in him that on occasion shone right through his skin, the white skin of his breast below the burn-line his singlet left. She could not bear it. She battered at him.

'Hey, *hey*,' he'd say, holding her off.

He had no idea what people were after. What she was after. What she saw in him.

David Malouf

For all the dire predictions among the clan, the doubts and amused speculations, they lasted; two people who, to the puzzlement of others, remained passionately absorbed in one another. Then one day she got a call at work. He had had a fall and was concussed again. Then in a coma, on a life-support system, and for four days and nights she was constantly at his side.

For part of that time she sat in a low chair and tuned her ear to a distant tinkling, as a breeze reached her, from far off over the edge of the world, and rolled a spent light bulb this way and that on a glass tabletop. She watched, fascinated. Hour after hour, in shaded sunlight and then in the blue of a hospital night lamp, the fragile sphere rolled, and she heard, in the depths of his skull, a clink of icebergs, and found herself sitting, half frozen, in a numbed landscape with not even a memory now of smell or taste or of any sense at all; only what she caught of that small sound, of something broken in a hermetic globe. To reach it, she told herself, I will have to smash the glass. And what then? Will the sound swell and fill me or will it stop altogether?

Meanwhile she listened. It demanded all her attention. It was a matter of life and death. When she could no longer hear it—

At other times she walked. Taking deep breaths of the hot air that swirled around her, she walked, howling, through the streets. Barefoot. And the breaths she took were to feed her howling. Each outpouring of sound emptied her lungs so completely that she feared she might simply rise up and float. But the weight of her bones, of the flesh that covered them, of the waste in her bowels, and her tears, kept her anchored—as did the invisible threads that tied her body to his, immobile under the crisp white sheet, its head swathed in bandages, and the wires connecting him to his other watcher, the dial-faced machine. It was his name she was howling. Mitch, she called. Sometimes Skip. At other times, since he did not respond to either of these, that other, earlier name he had gone by. Bobby, Bobby Kohler. She saw him, from where she was standing under the drooping leaves of a eucalypt at the edge of a track, running round the far side of an oval, but he was too deeply intent on his body, on his breathing, on the swing of his arms, the pumping of his thighs, to hear her.

Bobby, she called. Skip, she called. Mitch. He did not respond.

And she wondered if there was another name he might respond to that she had never heard. She tried to guess what it might be, certain now that if she found it, and called, he would wake. She found herself once leaning over him with her hands on his shoulders, prepared—was she mad?—to *shake* it out of him.

And once, in a moment of full wakefulness, she began to sing, very softly, in a high far voice, the tune he played on the ukulele. She had no words for it. Watching him, she thought he stirred. The slightest movement of his fingers. A creasing of the brow. Had she imagined it?

On another occasion, on the third or fourth day, she woke to find she had finally emerged from herself, and wondered—in the other order of time she now moved in—how many years had passed. She was older, heavier, her hair was grey, and this older, greyer self was seated across from her wearing the same intent, puzzled look that she too must be wearing. Then the figure smiled.

No, she thought, if that is me, I've become another woman altogether. Is that what time does to us?

It was the night they came and turned off the machine. His next of kin, his mother, had given permission.

Two days later, red-eyed from sleeplessness and bouts of uncontrollable weeping, she drove to Castle Hill for the funeral.

His mother had rung. She reminded Jo in a kindly voice that they had spoken before. Yes, Jo thought, like this. On the phone, briefly. When she had called once or twice at an odd hour and asked him to come urgently, she needed him, and at holiday times when he went dutifully and visited, and on his birthday. 'Yes,' Jo said. 'In June.' No, his mother told her, at the hospital. Jo was surprised. She had no memory of this. But when they met she recognized the woman. They *had* spoken. Across his hospital bed, though she still had no memory of what had passed between them. She felt ashamed. Grief, she felt, had made her wild; she still looked wild. Fearful now of appearing to lay claim to the occasion, she drew back and tried to stay calm.

The woman, Mitch's mother, was very calm, as if she had behind her a lifetime's practice of preserving herself against an excess of grief. But she was not ungiving.

'I know how fond Bobby was of you,' she told Jo softly. 'You must come and see me. Not today. Ring me later in the week. I can't have anyone at the house today. You'll understand why.'

Jo thought she understood but must have looked puzzled.

'Josh,' she said. 'I've got Josh home.' And Jo realized that the man standing so oddly close, but turned slightly away from them, was actually with the woman.

'I can't have him for more than a day or so at a time,' the woman was saying. 'He doesn't mean to be a trouble, and he'd never do me any harm, but he's so strong—I can't handle him. He's like a five-year-old. But a forty-year-old man has a lot of strength in his lungs.' She said this almost with humour. She reached out and squeezed the man's hand. He turned, and then Jo saw.

Large-framed and heavy-looking—hulking was the word that came to her—everything that in Mitch had been well knit and easy was, in him, merely loose. His hands hung without occupation at the end of his arms, the features in the long large face seemed unfocused, unintegrated. Only with Mitch in mind could you catch, in the full mouth, the heavy jaw and brow, a possibility that had somehow failed to emerge, or been maimed or blunted. The sense she had of sliding likeness and unlikeness was alarming. She gave a cry.

'Oh,' the woman said. 'I thought you knew. I thought he'd told you.'

Jo recovered, shook her head, and just at that moment the clergyman came forward, nodded to Mitch's mother, and they moved away to the open grave.

They were a small crowd. Most of them she knew. They were the members of the clan. The others, she guessed from their more formal clothes, must be relatives or family friends.

The service was grim. She steeled herself to stay calm. She had no wish to attract notice, to be singled out because she and Mitch had been—had been what? What had they been? She wanted to stand and be shrouded in her grief. To remain hidden. To have her grief, and him, all to herself as she had had him all to herself at least sometimes, many times, when he was alive.

But she was haunted now by the large presence of this other, this brother who stood at the edge of the grave beside his mother, quiet enough, she saw, but oddly unaware of what was going on about him.

He had moments of attention, a kind of vacant attention, then fell into longer periods of giant arrest. Then his eye would be engaged.

By the black fringe on the shawl of the small woman to his left, which he reached out for and fingered, frowning, then lifted to his face and sniffed.

By a wattlebird that was animating the branches of a low-growing grevillea so that it seemed suddenly to have developed a life of its own and began twitching and shaking out its blooms. Then by the cuff of his shirt, which he regarded quizzically, his mouth pouting, then drawn to one side, as if by something there that disappointed or displeased him.

All these small diversions that took his attention took hers as well. At such a moment! She was shocked.

Then, quite suddenly, he raised his head. Some new thing had struck him. What? Nothing surely that had been said or was being done here. Some thought of his own. A snatch of music it might be, a tune that opened a view in him that was like sunlight flooding a familiar landscape. His face was irradiated by a foolish but utterly beatific smile, and she saw how easy it might be—she thought of his mother, even more poignantly of Mitch—to love this large unlovely child.

The little ukulele tune came into her head, and with it a vision of Mitch, lost to her in his own world of impenetrable grief. Sitting in his underpants on the floor, one big foot propped on his thigh. Hunched over the strings and plucking from them, over and over, the same spare notes, the same bare little tune. And she understood with a pang how the existence of this spoiled other must have seemed like a living reproach to his own too easy attractiveness. It was that— the injustice of it, so cruel, so close—that all those nicks and scars and broken bones and concussions, and all that reckless exposure to a world of accident, had been meant to annul. She felt the ground shifting under her feet. How little she had grasped or known. What a different story she would have to tease out now and tell herself of their time together.

The service was approaching its end. The coffin, suspended on ropes, tilted over the hole with its raw edges and siftings of loose soil. It began, lopsidedly, to descend. Her eyes flooded. She closed them tight. Felt herself choke.

At that moment there was a cry, an incommensurate roar that made all heads turn and stopped the clergyman in full spate.

Some animal understanding—caught from the general emotion around him and become brute fact—had brought home to Josh what it was they were doing here. He began to howl, and the sound was so terrible, so piteous, that all Jo could think of was an animal at the most uncomprehending extreme of physical agony. People looked naked, stricken. There was a scrambling over broken lumps of earth round the edge of the grave. The big man, even in the arms of his mother, was uncontrollable. He struck out, face congested, the mouth and nose streaming, like an ox, Jo thought, like an ox under the hammer. And this, she thought, is the real face of grief, the one we do not show. Her heart was thick in her breast. This is what sorrow is that knows no explanation or answer. That looks down into the abyss and sees only the unanswering depths.

She recalled nothing of the drive back, through raw unfinished suburbs, past traffic lights where she must dutifully have swung into the proper lane and stopped, her mind in abeyance, the motor idling. When she got home, to the house afloat on its stilts among the sparse leaves of the coral trees, above the cove with its littered beach, she was drained of resistance. She sat in the high open space the house made, feeling it breathe like a living thing, surrendering herself to the regular long expansions of its breath.

Against the grain of her own need for what was enclosed and safe, she had learned to live with it. What now? Could she bear, alone, now that something final had occurred, to live day after day with what was provisional, which she had put up with till now because, with a little effort of adjustment, she too, she found, could live in the open present—so long as it *was* open.

Abruptly she rose, stood looking down for a moment at some bits of snipped wire, where he had been tinkering with something electrical, that for a whole week had lain scattered on the coffee table, then went out to the sink, and as on that first morning washed up what was there to be washed. The solitary cup and saucer from her early-morning tea.

For a moment afterwards she stood contemplating the perfection of clean plates drying in the rack, cups turned downward to drain, their saucers laid obliquely atop. She was at the beginning again. Or so she felt. Now what?

There was a sock on the floor. Out of habit she retrieved it, then stood, surveying the room, the house, as you could because it was so open and exposed.

Light and air came pouring in from all directions. She felt again, as on that first occasion, the urge to move in and begin setting things to rights, and again for the moment held back, restrained herself.

She looked down, observed the sock in her hand, and had a vision, suddenly, of the place as it might be a month from now when her sense of making things right would already, day after day, imperceptibly, have been at work on getting rid of the magazines and newspapers, shifting this or that piece of furniture into a more desirable arrangement, making the small adjustments that would erase all sign of him, of Mitch, from what had been so much of his making—from her life. Abruptly she threw the sock from her and stood there, shivering, hugging herself, in the middle of the room. Then, abruptly, sat where she had been sitting before. In the midst of it.

So what did she mean to do? Change nothing? Leave everything just as it was? The out-of-date magazines, that dead match beside the leg of the coffee table, the bits of wire, the sock? To gather fluff over the weeks and months, a dusty tribute that she would sit in the midst of for the next twenty years?

She sat a little longer, the room darkening around her, filling slowly with the darkness out there that lay over the waters of the cove, rose up from the floaty leaves of the coral trees and the shadowy places at their roots, from around the hairy stems of tree ferns and out of the unopened buds of morning glory. Then, with a deliberate effort, she got down on her knees and reached in to pick up the match from beside the leg of the coffee table. Shocked that it weighed so little. So little that she might not recall, later, the effort it had cost her, this first move towards taking up again, bit by bit, the weight of her life.

Then, with the flat of her hand, she brushed the strands of wire into a heap, gathered them up, and went, forcing herself, to retrieve the sock, then found the other. Rolled them into a ball and raised it to her lips. Squeezing her eyes shut, filling her nostrils with their smell.

Then there were his shirts, his shorts, his jeans—they would go to the Salvos—and the new things she had bought, which lay untouched in the drawers of his lowboy, the shirts in their plastic wrappers, the underpants, the socks still sewn or clipped together. Maybe Josh. She had a vision of herself arriving with these things on his mother's doorstep. An opening. The big man's pleasure as he stroked the front of his new poplin shirt, the sheen of its pure celestial blue.

She sat again, the small hoard of the rolled socks in her lap, the spent match and the strands of wire in a tidy heap. A beginning. And let the warm summer dark flow in around her. □

GRANTA

HELP, HELP, HELP
Jonathan Taylor

There is a moment—sometime in distant 1982—a moment we all remember—when, standing near the desk of a Saturday-morning group called The Explorers for talented, chess-playing children like my elder brother and their miscellaneous, tag-along siblings like myself— there is a moment—a moment which now makes my hair stand up on the back of my neck, but which, for years afterwards, was just a fascinating Sunday-dinner anecdote—a moment when my father, at this point still working, still raven-haired, still physically able to smile, forgot my baby sister's name—like a paper shred gusted away—and with a laugh and perhaps somewhere a vertiginous panic, had to grab my sleeve and ask what it was. The name he was looking for was his daughter's: Helen. I didn't understand quickly enough, didn't help.

The memory, like so many others, may mean nothing except in retrospect, but I still feel the tug on my shirt as he lunged towards me. 'My mind just went blankety-blank,' he'd say when someone brought up the story over cauliflower cheese. Was this the first inkling, we wonder now—was this the first one-way street his mind mistakenly turned up?

But there are many other possible first inklings, some of them lost in the dead ends of *my* memory. My father had Parkinson's disease with associated dementia: illnesses so gradual, so much a continuum of greyness, that one can only properly remember the most recent state—which now is death. All I can provide are fragments of memories—a list of vanishing points and partial origins.

May 1983: I was nearly ten years old, my father was fifty-five. Apart from some nasty bullying (which persisted throughout my school years like the weather), I don't remember anything particularly startling about that spring—even though my father was in the process of quitting his headmastership, having a nervous breakdown and maybe contemplating serious self-harm. My mother had to ask my elder brother to 'keep a careful eye on Dad' whenever she went to the shops, in case razors, pills or knives were put to an alternative use. My father had been put on Amitriptyline (an antidepressant), on which he was dependent until 1989. He was also sent to regular sessions with a psychiatrist.

I don't recall noticing any of these things. Perhaps it seemed that my mother put her hair in curlers slightly more often at this time—

a sure indication that she was in a fraught mood—but, otherwise, nothing. It seems incredible to me now: how blind, insensitive, stupid was I, that a father's nervous breakdown could pass me by?

Except that there was one thing, there was one afternoon, as I clambered up the stairs, my parents' bedroom door open in front of me, overhearing, as I reached the top step, my father on the phone, saying, 'Yes, I've decided to change my mind and accept the early retirement offer you made'—and then scampering back down the stairs, knowing that I'd heard something I shouldn't have, feeling that what I'd done was wrong, but not able to tell a soul, however excited I was at the thought of my father staying at home. A few weeks later, the second sign of his retirement appeared: an electric Teasmade (one of those Eighties, quiz-show prizes which made tea for you when the alarm went off). What a lavish leaving-present for eleven years' service as headmaster of the toughest school in Stoke-on-Trent. Thirty-four years' work as a teacher = a Teasmade, which also = ten minutes on a second-rate quiz show—this was a simple simultaneous equation, like the ones my father used to help me with. To my frustration, the Teasmade stayed in the box, despite my insensitive, childish fascination. It eventually merged with the attic dust.

August 1987: Friends of my computer and myself come over to play. My brother puts his head round the study door to shout, 'Computer boffins!' at us, and then runs off; my little sister comes in to show my friends her guinea pig, so it can wee on them; my dad wanders in to ask us if we want a cup of tea or anything (non-alcoholic, of course) to drink. Then he shuffles off. Sometimes he comes back an hour later to ask if we want a cup of tea or anything to drink. Sometimes he doesn't come back at all. Sometimes he comes with the wrong things balanced precariously on an Isle of Man tea-tray, biscuits swimming in what's been spilled. The first time my friends laugh and say to me, 'You ask your dad for a cup of tea one day and you get an orange squash next week—the only thing slower than his tea-making is his driving.' I laugh too. The second time my friends laugh and say to me, 'You ask for a cup of tea at your house and you get it next month.' I laugh with them, swearing to myself that I won't laugh next time—that I'll put up a fight. The third time my friends laugh and say to me, 'You ask for a cup of tea and a jammy dodger at your house and your dad goes off and milks the fucking cow.' I smile and stay quiet as he comes into the room, slightly lopsided, like a faulty Teasmade.

June 1988: My father's awkwardness, shakiness, lethargy, slow driving, forgetfulness, depression, nightmares and tea-making are all lumped together and diagnosed by a young neurologist looking for medals: 'I know what you've got!' he exclaims proudly. No one else knows. No one else found it out. Just him. My father's condition is at the extreme end of the spectrum of Parkinson's disease, partly because it is 'early onset' Parkinson's; he's only sixty years old and Parkinson's is usually an old person's disease, as if that makes it better.

I'm sure most father–son, mother–daughter relationships are shot through with trivial micro-battles: microscopic victories and defeats over coffee-making, bathroom-tidying, car-cleaning. The problem for me, though, was that, as my father's illness encroached, I started winning all the time; and that's not healthy for anyone, let alone a teenager. A bit of a pushover, you might say, lapping someone with Parkinson's, who spends most of the day asleep in an armchair.

Take the washing-up. By the time I was sixteen, I was offering to clean the dishes after tea to please my mother. Such a 'good Boy'. (My father used to call me 'Boy' after Boy in the old Johnny Weissmuller *Tarzan* films; he thought I looked like him.) I'd fill the bowl with soapy water while my father cleared the table. Often, the clink of the plates would merge with a lecture about Charles XII of Sweden or Louis XIV of France. I was studying A-level History, and he was trying to persuade me that it wasn't a big yawn: 'When I get you talking about it, Boy, you chatter away enthusiastically. So I don't understand why you always complain about it.'

'I'm not the one chattering about it,' I mutter.

'Pardon?'

'Nothing.'

'Pardon?'

'It was nothing. Just bring me the stuff off the table, will you? I've had enough of Charles XII for one day.' That was how I treated and ended some of the last, extended conversations we ever had. He knew everything (or so it seems to me now) and I asked him, talked to him, about nothing.

Reduced to silence, he'd bring a pile of cups from the table and slide them into the washing-up bowl in front of me.

'Dad!'

'What?'

'Dad!'

'What?'

'I've told you not to put the stuff straight into the bowl.'

'It doesn't matter.'

'I've told you before. I rinse the food off the plates first.'

Pause. Some of the stew rises to the top with the bubbles.

'Look what you've... Dad!' He's done it again, sliding dishes with bits of banana jelly straight into the water. There are bubbles of beef jelly and banana stew in front of me.

'I can't believe it. I told you this second. And you've done it again. You did it on purpose'—this is quite possible.

'I forgot'—this is, of course, even more possible.

'No, you didn't.'

'Stop making a fuss about nothing.'

'I won't. You can do the washing up now. You can finish it.'

My mother comes into the kitchen: 'What's the noise for? What have you done, darling?' Me: 'He put the dirty washing-up straight in the bowl.' Mum: 'Oh, darling. You know the others don't like that. You know they don't wash up like you, with it all swimming in a big mess.' Me: 'I'd told him once and he did it again.' Dad: 'I forgot.' Mum: 'For goodness' sake, darling. Can't you do anything right?' Me: 'He can finish it. I'm not doing it like that.' I storm out of the room, hearing my mother behind me: 'Look what you've done. You've upset him again.' My father, defeated, shouts: 'Don't you see? It's just his excuse to get angry at me and not do the job he's meant to do.' Mum: 'Don't be silly, darling. You're so cynical about them.'

I confess. I confess that my father's cynical 'silliness' about me, about the washing-up, about a million tiny things, was often right. I confess my teenage laziness and point-scoring: I did just want an excuse to get angry with him and get out of the washing up, an excuse which made me look like the injured party and made my mother side with me over him.

I could resort to another excuse to excuse these past excuses. I could point out that it wasn't easy growing up while my father was growing down with Parkinson's. But no. Some of it was all too easy, especially the point-scoring. I will confess without excuses: growing up was a million micro-battles which I kept winning. My father was the opposition, my mother kept the score.

By the time I'd reached my twenties, 'help' was the word my mother probably heard more than any other.

With his eyes screwed shut, his head hunched forwards and his left arm outstretched, my father would shake his chair, shouting 'Help' and hitting the wall behind him in some kind of syncopated drum-and-bass rhythm ('help bang help bang help help bang'). He'd do this even if we were all in the room and there was nothing visibly wrong. The call for help wasn't necessarily a demand for any particular object—my father just wanted some unspecified and, in the end, unrealizable help of some or all kinds. It was one of the only ways he had left to communicate with the world. For that reason, we shouldn't have begrudged him the word so much.

'Help.' There were countless ways he could cry out: desperate wail, psychopathic whisper, Wagnerian fortissimo, Puccinian heart-wrench, Gilbert-and-Sullivanian patter ('helphelphelphelpmehelphelphelpmehelp'), minimalist chug, Beatlesian urgency ('Help, I need somebody')...

In a different form, the point-scoring continued when I started looking after him in my mother's absence. 'Wait till Mum gets home'—as opposed to the more familiar 'Wait till your father gets home'—was the threat I used if he was 'playing up'. When my mother did get home, I would rehearse the incidents that day—and his failings—in gory detail. She would say: 'Oh dear, what has he done today?' and I would answer, 'What hasn't he done today? He kept shouting and trying to fall out of his chair. He threw a cup of tea on the floor. Then he fell on the broken pieces. On purpose. The cuts are his fault, not mine. He wouldn't get up. When I'd cleaned him up, he went to the toilet a thousand and one times. Then he... Then he... Then he really started annoying me...'

One girlfriend who overheard me talk like this told me I was a bastard. I was supposed to be looking after him, not scoring points against him, she said. And of all people, your mother doesn't want to hear it. You're just making her feel guilty for leaving him with you.

I agreed, but tried to explain. I tried to explain that I needed someone to register every single, tiny detail of the day. Otherwise, what happened between my father and I was effectively non-existent; after all, he couldn't register it, remember it, one minute to the next. I tried to explain that I needed to justify my exhaustion, my frustration, and—if things had got out of hand—my fury to someone. In return, I needed that someone to exclaim gratefully, 'There, there, never mind, you did well, you tried your best, thank you, thank you.' That someone could only be my mother; it was impossible to describe what went on to anyone else.

It's May 1995 and I'm cross. In a test conducted this morning on my father, he has just failed to distinguish between a photo of me and a photo of Humphrey Bogart. This might have been flattering, had he not then gone on to mistake Bogart for a giraffe and ultimately everything for everything else. A doctoral student from Birmingham University has been visiting for months now, collecting data about my father's condition for a research paper. 'He just didn't want to play today,' says my mother, nonchalantly shoving a handful of colourful pills into his mouth and then pinning his head back with a glass of water. The student has already left, but my mother is worried that my father's unwillingness 'to play' will mess up the poor girl's research results. 'Last week, he managed to identify the photos well until he switched off but today he just wasn't in the mood.'

I reassure her—the student probably wants 'bad' results anyway. They'll make the research look more interesting. And I'm right. Years later, after his death, I happen across the research paper the student published about my relationship with my father: 'Delusional Misidentification: A Neuropsychological Case Study in Dementia Associated with Parkinson's Disease'. In it, my father is 'Case 1' and I'm 'Junior'. Retrospectively, I find out that Case 1 suffered from a form of dementia called Lewy body dementia, and a peculiar variant of Capgras syndrome whereby he misidentified Jnr and believed he was being impersonated or even taken over by a villainous double. Case 1's Capgras, I discover, also involved elements of 'Fregoli' and 'intermetamorphosis' syndromes, both of which involve the misrecognition of a stranger as a 'significant other'. My father's form of misrecognition, the writer suggests, is a peculiar one which blurs the boundaries between Capgras, Fregoli and intermetamorphosis syndromes, demanding a rethink of these terms. 'Typical Dad,' comments my mother on reading the article. 'Even his delusions had to be different from everyone else's.'

It's hard for me to grasp, but I find there are sections of the brain—in the right hemisphere—which are devoted to processing, sorting and recognizing faces. Thus damage of the right hemisphere might mean damage of this processing system. You can read about such things in the great book by Oliver Sacks, *The Man Who Mistook His Wife for a Hat*. Who knows which is worse: being mistaken for a villainous double or for an inanimate hat?

Whichever, they're both caused by specifically biological processes in the brain—The Man Who Mistook His Wife for a Hat, for example, did so because of a massive tumour. Imagine that (if it's possible to imagine it): your ability or inability to differentiate faces and to know to whom they belong is a biological function, is built into the material of your brain. What does that mean for supposedly spiritual or mental concepts like 'love' and 'hate'? Does it mean that the kind of serial monogamist we all know, who transfers his or her love all too easily from one partner to another, has a weak facial recognition processor, so that lovers become interchangeable? Does it mean that racism might be a neurological syndrome? When an unregenerate member of the BNP says, 'They all look the same,' is this just because his or her right hemisphere is damaged?

For my father, one of the routes to the facial processor had become impaired by disease. And the result was that I was no longer me. Instead, the double—the body-snatcher—who had tyrannically taken over my body and face was a deputy at his old school whom he hadn't got on with. Let's call him Gil-Martin for the sake of this story, after the famous doppelgänger in James Hogg's *The Private Memoirs and Confessions of a Justified Sinner*.

I had no conception of these things at the time, no knowledge of the theories, the different syndromes. I didn't even know who had so discourteously snatched my body, wasn't really aware my body had been snatched (but then, neither do people in science-fiction films). I was merely aware that certain symptoms were occurring and that I didn't recognize the person my father recognized as me. He was furious at me, shrank from me, shrieked for help when I was there, and I didn't know why. I just thought that he was confused and took me for some generalized baddie, or (worse) that he did recognize me and no longer liked what he saw. And I couldn't always blame him for that—sometimes I myself didn't like the tyrant his incessant 'Help!'s teased out of me.

I didn't realize that in my father's mind, someone else's face was tyrannizing mine. Years later, over a croissant, I asked my mother why it was my face, in particular, which was the one tyrannized by misidentification. And she told me it was just because both the deputy and I had long, straggly hair. What a let-down, I thought. What a paltry cause for something so bizarre, so science-fictionish. I had known that my father never liked my hippy hair, but not that it was a major cause of his delusions. Why didn't anyone tell me at the time? I could easily have had it cut to cure him.

Meanwhile, back in 1995, my father pushes away the glass that my mother is holding to his mouth.

'What was that for?' she demands.

He keeps pushing at her, bouncing in the chair to get up.

'It was him!' he says, pointing at me. 'He did it!'

'Don't be ridiculous, and stop pushing me,' says my mother. 'I've got to finish making tea. You need to stay sitting for a while. Watch the television or you'll fall.'

'No—not while *he's* around!' I can still remember the stress on any pronouns referring to me (whoever I was at the time) when he was in this frame of mind. Almost by definition, pronouns invite misidentification. They can so easily slip from one person to another, allowing the mind to slip with them. My father never used proper nouns when he was angry or paranoiac.

Now, though, his anger has started trailing off into tiredness: 'He's out to get me... I tell you what he was doing. He...he was...' A loud advert on the television for conservatories supervenes, and consequently he finishes his sentence with the peculiar accusation that I was 'building an Edwardian-style porch with double...double...double-gla...zing...' He yawns, we laugh, and within a few minutes, he's sitting down on the chair again, drooling and snoring, while I crash away at the piano on the other side of the room. He only wakes once to point and laugh at the pink goats he sees sitting next to my elbow, and who are accompanying me with complex harmonies.

Then there's a loud noise from the television and he comes to, muttering something over and over about a teacher collecting the schoolchildren from the playground. Eventually, there's a crescendo to 'Help help help help help help'—and it is more desperate, more insistent this time.

'Help with what?' I ask, suspending my piano-playing.

'Help.'

'You want help with help?' = facetious winding up.

'Go away—I don't want you... It's not you.'

'What do you want?' = aggressive impatience.

'I want your mum.' Bang bang bang bang bang bang bang.

'Stop doing that.' I saunter over to him and move his hand back on to his lap. 'Don't disturb her. She's busy, don't you know?' = authoritative self-righteousness.

'Help.'

'She's cooking tea. She can't come at your beck and call' = more self-righteousness.

'Help help help help help. Help help help. Erm'—he seems momentarily to lose his thread, and then recovers it: 'Help.'

'Come on, Dad, be reasonable' = pretend imploration.

'No. Help help help help. Get him away from me.' Bang bang bang bang bang bang bang bang bang bang. 'You've got to get the pupils in from break.'

'You're at home, Dad. You've been retired years. You don't have to worry about that sort of thing any more' = patronizing reassurance.

'Help! Help! Get that person away from me.' Bang bang bang bang bang bang bang.

I take hold of his hand to stop its machinic thumping of the door. He wraps his fingers round mine in a grip which would crack walnuts. So weak and clumsy and fragile, yet he has what the doctors call a 'prehensile grip'—as if his out-of-control body is somehow flashing back to the strength of nut-cracking, tree-swinging gibbons. I can feel that grip now; somehow, somewhere, the bruises remain.

'I want to go home.'

'You're at home—in your own sitting room.'

'I want to go home. Help help help help.'

'Oh, for God's sake… Come on, Dad.' As usual, I'm starting to laugh, and I don't know why. It's a kind of reflex action, no different from crying.

'What's going on here, then? What are you up to, darling?' asks my mother as she comes in through the door, wiping her hands on an Isle of Man tea towel.

'It's always me. You always take his side. It's not me. It's him—that person.' He jabs an accusing finger at me with his spare hand.

'That's Jonathan, your son,' says my mother.

'No, it's not. It's not. Can't you see? It's that fraud, playing tricks on me.'

Not knowing what reaction I should have, I laugh again; my mother laughs too.

My father pushes at me, as if trying to expel whoever I am from his past. But he's unable to release his own grip, unable to let go of something he himself is grasping. He's stuck in the violent but impotent rage of dreams. 'It's this…sod—that's what he is, I tell you.'

I'm still laughing, and my laughter sends his fury spiralling upwards, exponentially. His grip tightens.

'I don't hear language like that,' my mother says.

'Help.'

'Come on now, darling. That's enough.'

'Help.'

'Come on, now.'

'Help.'

'What do you want anyway?'

'He doesn't want anything.' I say this to wind my father up further, knowing it's not true.

'I want to go home. It's him—he's kidnapped me. He's taken me and kidnapped me. I tell you—he's…' His fury's too much to allow him to finish the sentence. Instead, he shouts, 'It's him…he's been like it ever since he came to the school, ever since he…' and he finishes the sentence by flailing at me again. He stares with wide-eyed paranoia at us.

'Gosh, look at that face,' comments my mother, and we both smile down at a face paralysed into a scowl. There's a silent horror movie from the 1920s where a clown is mutilated when young; afterwards, all he can do is grin, even when he is murderously unhappy.

Parkinson's does the opposite, gradually petrifying your facial muscles into those of a miserable, wrinkled, growling clown. This is what's known as 'masking'. Day in, day out, my father had to watch us smiling and laughing, while he couldn't join in.

Every word, every phrase, every sentence, every everything had to be repeated over and over again to my father, just as my father himself repeated actions over and over again. I can't put down here the amount of repetition involved; it would be a waste of trees. But for the carers as for the sufferer, Parkinson's and dementia seem to me to be all about repetition, and the repetition of repetition.

Obviously, as regards dementia, there's going to be a hell of a lot of repetition since you forget what you've said, or what you've been told, from one minute to the next. A million different moments might be cited as examples: 'Where did you say my jumper with reindeers on was?' 'In the top drawer.' Pause. 'Where did you say my jumper with the reindeers on was?' 'In the top drawer.' Pause. 'Have you found it yet?' 'What?' 'The jumper with the reindeers on.' 'No, where is it?' 'In the top drawer.' 'What's in the top drawer?' 'The jumper with the reindeers on.' 'Why do I want a jumper with reindeers on?' 'Because it's Christmas.' 'What's Christmas?'

Similarly, in terms of Parkinson's, many of the recognized, neurological symptoms are based on automatic repetition. They have beautiful-sounding names: palilalia is the repetition of words; palipraxia is the repetition of physical actions; echopraxia is the repetition of other people's actions; and the most magical-sounding of all, echolalia, is just my father automatically repeating 'let go let go let go' after we've said it to him a dozen times. I didn't know about these neurological symptoms in 1995 but since I've found out I've suddenly started seeing palilalia, palipraxia, echopraxia and echolalia everywhere: in shops and pubs, at parties, on buses, in classrooms, symphonies, novels.

Looking back, these compulsive repetitions echoed from patient to carers (and back again): lift him up, sit him down, lift him up, sit him down, sit him back, untwist his emaciated legs, relax his shaking arms, untwist his legs, relax his arms, make him drink some pop, make him eat some food, make him drink some pop, teeth in, teeth out…and so on and so on, as if the carers reflect the patient in a hall of mirrors, a hall of echolalias and echopraxias. A simple 'let go' or 'open your eyes' or 'stand up' becomes 'let go let go let go let go' or 'open your eyes open your eyes open your bloody eyes' or 'stand up stand up stand up for fuck's sake you're breaking my back stand up'. It's not just the sufferer whose syntax breaks down: you, the carer, have to repeat everything without punctuation, without let up, in the same tone over and over, and try not to lose patience…

And the point of all this repetition? Well, as far as my father was concerned, it wasn't necessarily—or wasn't just—to try and cajole him into doing something, in the hope that, if said enough times, the message would get through. Just because you repeat an order two or three times to a waiter who doesn't speak English doesn't mean they'll understand you better. Oh no. All that repetition was there to fill time, to feel we were doing something while we were really just waiting for the symptoms to change: for one of the pill cycles to kick in or kick out, for the fidgeting to stop, for the muscles to relax or get going, for him to open his eyes or fall asleep—for him to capitulate to our wishes without input from his own volition.

'Care' involves frustration as well as patience, violence—mental and physical, for both sufferer and carer—as well as benevolence, so-called. Perhaps only other carers can understand that. Or perhaps only my mother. Personally, I'll confess to anyone willing to listen that I hit my father on occasion—sometimes before, sometimes after he hit me.

'But he hit me,' my father would say, after being subjected to my recital of his misdemeanours.

'I don't blame him. He says you've been playing up, darling. It's not on. He says you fell over, and broke a pint of milk, and fell over again, and shouted, and hurt his back. This won't do, darling. We can't go on like this.'

'Lies! All bloody lies! He's just scoring points by listing lies. It's him. He did those things, I tell you, not me!'

'Come on, darling. You can't keep behaving like this.'

He pauses, and glances between us with wide eyes: 'I see. You both. In a conspiracy. You both together, out to get me. He's out to get me. And you're on his side. Why don't you…why don't you go off with him if that's what you want? Go off with your…your fancy man.'

I laugh, embarrassed. Now I want to give back the points I've scored by listing his faults. My mother shoves him into the chair and snaps: 'Be quiet, darling, and don't be silly. Here, it's time for your pills.'

'I... He... I... You together... Conspiracy...' He trails off, losing the thread of his paranoia, his mouth stuffed with tablets.

Paranoia. Odd word, that. It implies that the paranoiac is necessarily wrong or mad; etymologically, the word comes from the Greek, via Latin, for 'distracted', from *para* 'beyond' and *noos* 'mind'. I'm sure a lot of people who live with a paranoiac, however, feel quietly guilty, concerned that the paranoiac is more right than mad. In this sense, paranoia is a contagious disease: the carer gradually becomes paranoid that the paranoiac isn't paranoid but has got a point. I became paranoid that my father's paranoia was a bit close to the mark—that he recognized me all too well for the Oedipal point-scorer I was.

I can't help worrying that my behaviour shaped and even caused his paranoia, at least to some extent. On the one hand, there was his (frequently correct) cynicism about me: he saw through my washing-up scams, while my mother didn't. Perhaps he'd done the same when he was young and knew the tricks. On the other hand, he must have felt a terrible frustration at his decreasing ability to make his opinion count for anything but 'silliness': 'Don't be silly, darling. It's just the disease speaking.' Did the latter compound the former over and over again? Did cynicism become paranoia? And did paranoia become misidentification, transforming me into that arch-villain Mr Gil-Martin? Is there a graph I could draw, an equation I could formulate, to express the gradual transformation from son to Gil-Martin? Cynicism + Frustration, both raised to the power of 1,000,000 micro-battles = Paranoia + Capgras misidentification.

I remember a trip into town with my parents in 1993. Standing in WH Smith, I flick through the CDs and pick one out. It's a new recording of Mahler's Seventh Symphony, with a beautiful illustration by Charles Rennie Mackintosh called *Harvest Moon* on the cover. My father's at my elbow.

'Looks good, doesn't it?' I say.

'Hmm. I don't go for this Mahler chap like you do. It's a fad, if you ask me, like flares.' He pauses, as if he's forgotten what he was saying but has remembered something else, something more important. 'Boy, do you want that?'

'What?'

'Do you want it? I'll get that Mahler for you.' His fingers have closed round the other side of the CD from mine. He's not looking at his hand, though, because he doesn't need to; at the moment, it's performing its function on its own, smoothly and unconsciously. He's looking straight at me. His other hand is in his pocket, searching for his Visa card.

He can't find the words to say he knows what's happening when he answers the door and sees Gil-Martin instead of me. He can't find the words to say he wants to make his son feel better about everything. 'He never spoke very much,' my mother says, 'but it got worse with Parkinson's. He had fewer and fewer words left to speak with, less and less of a voice that wasn't a mumbly-whisper kind of thing.' But here he is in WH Smith, trying to recover something from the 'mumbly-whisper' the illness is gradually imposing. Here he is, trying to express himself, even if it's only through the language of Visa. If, at this moment, he can't find the words to convey that he knows I'm his son—and he knows his son likes Mahler—at least his Visa can.

But if my sinking feeling understands his Visa language minutes, months and years later, at the precise second it's happening, I miss one of his last acts of generosity. Instead, my reflex action is to say, 'No, it's okay. You mustn't,' and I take the CD from him and return it to the shelf. Perhaps I'm hoping he'll argue the point, but he doesn't respond at all—just grunts and wanders off, the shaking starting again, the moment lost.

There's a section of your brain, some scientists have stated recently, that is devoted to empathy. Empathy and sympathy are biological processes in what's known as the brain's 'mind-reading' faculty. It's this that allows us to comprehend, recognize, experience and sympathize with other people's emotions and personalities.

We exist in others only as the sum of the cells devoted to us in their amygdalae, superior temporal sulci, medial frontal cortices and orbito-frontal cortices—just as they exist in ours. You might open up someone else's brain and find a miniature version of yourself in there. But then again, you might not recognize the 'you' that's imprinted on his or her grey matter. In his later years, I certainly wouldn't have recognized my imprint in my father's 'mind-reading' faculty, given Capgras syndrome. And, I dare say, vice versa, too. I didn't have the excuse of Capgras, but it's said that some people—people with autism, for example—have damaged 'mind-reading' modules, which means they can't empathize or identify with others properly.

For years, I felt that my brain's 'mind-reading' capacity must be damaged or underdeveloped. Empathy's running low, I hear the scientists say. Maybe other faculties annexed empathy cells for their own purposes—the how-to-get-out-of-chores-faculty, for instance. On many occasions during my father's illness, I realized after the event that he and his Visa had been trying to say or do something fatherish ('let me buy you this CD as a present'). But I always missed these moments because they were camouflaged among ten thousand 'Help help help help help's, 'Who are you?'s and 'I told you so's. There were so many times when he tried his best to recognize me, and I was the one who ruined it with the wrong response ('No, it's okay. You mustn't').

Perhaps, I'd feel afterwards, perhaps if I'd answered correctly, he'd have answered me—and we would have had a proper conversation. Perhaps, by finding the right answer at the right time, he'd have forgotten his dementia, forgotten his forgetfulness, forgotten his tremors and terrors. But no. My empathy cells only worked in retrospect, after each opportunity had vanished. Like now. □

MRS COVET
Rebecca Miller

Mrs Covet

It started with the ladybugs.

The first one was a taste of luck on a spring day as I folded towels in the kids' bathroom. The shiny little bubble moved clumsily up the mirror, seemed actually to waddle in her red armour with its cheerful yellow spots.

Ladybug, Ladybug, fly away home, your children are crying,/Your house is on fire.

What's lucky about that?

I leaned over and put my finger up to her; she crawled up on it. I wondered, *Are you supposed to make a wish?*

Tyler walked in then, eyes puffy from his nap, and pulled down his pants for a pee, utterly unaware of my presence. I watched him, the ladybug balanced on my fingertip, as the manly stream of yellow piss thundered down into the bowl. He pulled his pants up and turned towards the door.

'What about your hands?' I said.

He turned to me and smiled, only mildly surprised to see me there, then held his chubby hands out for me to wash. I am as ubiquitous as air in this house for my children; often they take as much notice of me as if I were a breeze filtering through the screen door. This doesn't sound too good, I know, but I take pride in it. My kids trust me. They know I'll be there.

Tyler went back into his room. I heard him starting to build an airport. His older brother, Kyle, was still in school. It was two-thirty, and I figured I had time for a quick orgasm before school let out. So I went into our bedroom, slipped under the covers of the unmade bed, and took off my pants.

Un petit mort. That's what the French call it. A little death. It is like dying, isn't it? The open mouth, the closed eyes, and how you go out of time for a few seconds—you're nowhere. It's impossible to feel fear while you're coming. I wouldn't care if there were a shark charging at me through the surf.

When I first flirted with Craig in college, we were flipping through an anthology of French poems when we read it there and giggled. *Un petit mort.* Later, when we were in bed together, we whispered it into each other's ears—*un petit mort.* (We were French majors.)

Actual physical sex seems so clumsy and awkward to me these days. My own nudity seems rubbery, numb, this pregnant belly and thin weak limbs, rough shock of pubic hair. Sex works much more smoothly in my mind. I never think of anyone but my husband of course—that would be a real betrayal. I haven't ever been unfaithful to Craig, and I wouldn't. I always turn him into a stranger, though, when I do it: some guy I meet in a bar, or a library. He looks over at me and he just can't help being excited by my huge butt (which I actually do not have).

So I do kind of secretly understand those gay men who say they just love to make it with strangers. I mean, I would never have the courage personally to go pick up someone I hadn't even been introduced to, and I probably wouldn't even *like* it, if it were real. Or maybe I would. But you know how some people are so disgusted with the idea of certain gay men and how they used to have sex with strangers before Aids; who knows, maybe they still do, but not all of them do—in fact the most solid couple I know, aside from me and Craig, are both men—Larry and Dennis, we had them over to dinner last week. They wouldn't dream of picking up a stranger. I am totally non-homophobic—except of course when it comes to my sons, where it does make me mildly nervous, the idea of them being queers, but they're not, I don't think. It's probably too early to tell, though you think I'd have an intuition.

Anyway the point is, I think there is something sort of heartbreaking about sex with strangers. But at the same time I believe absolutely in fidelity. Because I just can't stand hurting people and I can't stand being hurt. I never wanted a dog—even as a kid— because dogs die after ten or thirteen years, at the most, and then you have to live through that loss again and again *with every dog.* They make you love them, they practically become a person to you, and then they die. Or they get so sick you actually have to have them killed. We had a dog when I was a little girl, a collie, her name was Folly, Folly the Collie, and one day when she was old she got frozen to the ice outside. She couldn't get up any more. It didn't help warming her up; her legs had gone. She looked up at us helplessly and my dad and I took her to the vet and I held her while they gave her the injection and she peeked up at me with a worried, obedient expression. She knew that I was going to kill her, and she didn't understand why. And then I was supposed to leave the room—or maybe I was scared to stay. I left Folly alone to die. So that was pretty terrible. And I have resisted getting my own boys pets for this reason. The price for love, we all know, is eventually loss, and it's a stiff price, let me tell you. Romantic movies and books are waging a perpetual ad campaign trying to get us all to love with unbridled passion. 'Love!' they say. 'Love! Love more! Abandon all precaution! Stop being so defensive! Feeling a chill in your marriage? Get a divorce! Marry the repairman!'

I haven't noticed any of the authors of these propaganda pieces putting their home phone numbers inside their book jackets or on the end credits of their films, so that we can call them when we have to go to the hospital and watch the people we have loved with such abandon *die*. They offer no help as we witness our husbands, wives, parents, children, turn blue and green and crumple up like an old balloon; I haven't noticed them offering to put away the garments of the dead, or those who have abandoned us for others. Where are these artists when we need them? Do they offer us any condolence whatsoever? No, because they don't care about us. They don't even think about us. They feed off of our yearning to be loved as totally as when we were at our mother's tit, they grow rich off of our pathetic need to be happy as embryos, bathed in the warm bath of our mother's blood.

About a week after I saw the first ladybug, I noticed there were five of them in the boys' bathroom. Two in the sink, one in the bathtub, two crawling around on the mirror. Days after that, I was reading Tyler a story in his bed when one of them dropped on to my cheek. It panicked me, I shrieked. I never knew they could fly. They land clumsily, stupidly, and when it's time to take off, they push a little secret pair of wings out from under their shells. Within a month I had counted thirty-five ladybugs in the boys' bathroom alone. Then I started finding them in the bedrooms, our bathroom, the closets. They were flying more and more, and one day one of them was zooming around in crazy circles, and it bit me in the back of the leg. It was an invasion. I started to think they were evil.

But you can't kill a ladybug. It's terrible luck to kill a ladybug.

I started spending more and more time out of the house. Once I dropped the boys at school, I stayed out, got a cup of decaf, went food shopping, even went to a matinee a couple of times. Then I would pick up Tyler from nursery school and we'd go out to an early lunch. The house was becoming a mess. Orange peels under the beds, grime in the toilet bowl. Craig tried to be nice about it. He knows how I get when I'm pregnant. It's hard to describe what happens—it's as though all the walls in my mind slide down like car windows, and the thoughts just float freely around my brain. I find socks in the freezer, notebooks in the linen closet. I once showed up two days late to the dentist. At least I got the time right. But the ladybugs were threatening to be a real problem. I couldn't sleep, I didn't want to be in the house, and I wouldn't let Craig get an exterminator. One night, we were sitting at the kitchen table after dinner. Craig watched as one of the creatures crawled along the edge of a bowl filled with coagulating breakfast cereal. Then he said, 'If you need help with the house, I'll get you someone. I'll ask my mother.' I burst into tears. I'm not sure if it was relief, or a premonition.

The very next day, at nine a.m., my mother-in-law, Carroll Rice, drove up in her Ford Impala. She was in baby blue: ironed slacks, matching blue sweater with shoulder pads in it. Her white-blonde hair had even taken on a bluish cast. Still in Craig's pyjamas, I watched her through the window, my belly pressing against the glass, as she got out of the car, primly brushing imaginary crumbs from her bust, and walked around to the other side. The passenger door opened with ominous slowness; I saw one hand grip the side of the doorframe. A dark head appeared, then swung out of view. A moment passed. Suddenly, an enormous woman heaved herself out of the low car and unfolded herself with difficulty. She must have been six feet tall. Short, dark hair, athletic build. Breasts the size of watermelons. Carroll came up to her shoulder. The two of them strode up to the house. Carroll opened the door with a perfunctory knock, calling out 'Daphne!' in her high, sing-song voice.

'Hi, Carroll,' I said. My underarms were sweating, my teeth were unbrushed, my hair snarled. Carroll looked me up and down and sighed. She'd had six kids and I doubt she'd let herself look like this for one single morning.

'Honey, this is Nat. She is going to get your life in order.'

The Enormous Woman towered over me. Her eyes were light,

piercing green; her massive chin seemed clamped on to the rest of her face by a fierce underbite. She was wearing a vast, pink terry-cloth sweatsuit. 'I hear you need a little help with the house,' she said.

'Well,' I said. 'I, I...think I do. We just thought we'd try...'

'You sit tight, honey,' Nat said. 'You don't look too good. I'm a trained nurse, so calm down.' I sat.

Carroll looked at me smugly. 'I am so glad you finally let me help you,' she whispered. Nat made us both tea, then set about cleaning the kitchen, whistling loudly, with vibrato. After a while, she thundered upstairs and turned the radio on. I never even showed her around the house. She figured it all out for herself.

Later, drying myself off from my shower, I could hear the sermon she was listening to on the radio. A man's voice was saying, 'But the question is not what *you* need. The question is: *What does Jesus need? And the answer is easy—because the answer is always the same: Jesus needs your love.*' By the time I emerged from my room, Nat had found a place for everything in the house. Anything that could fit inside another thing got crammed in there. It didn't matter if it made no sense. She put hair elastics inside egg cups. Magic markers in the salad bowl. The place looked immaculate, but a lot of things went missing.

After a day or two, I began to suspect that Nat was killing the ladybugs. There were fewer and fewer of them around. Once I found twenty dead bodies on a window sill. I sniffed, but I couldn't smell chemicals. Why were they dying? 'It's the end of their season,' said Nat. But still I suspected her. So many ladybugs ought to have brought something hugely lucky to our lives. Killing them could bring calamity. I started to fret and whenever I hadn't felt the baby move for more than an hour, I poked it till it squirmed.

Nat cooked, too. The fare was plain, fairly tasteless, but the kids loved it: lasagna, spaghetti with meatballs, fried fish, baked beans. After she was done with the cleaning on that first day, at around one, I expected her to leave, but all she did was put on an apron and start chopping. When the kids were home, she had them doing chores. Tyler walked around with a cleaning rag hanging from his belt, a sponge in one hand. Both boys loved working for Nat. She combed their tousled hair, tamed the curls I loved and slicked them back with water. She started talking about buzz cuts. With the house cleaned, the kids occupied, dinner in the oven, all I had to do was read and wait for Craig to come home. I spent more and more time in my room. Nat fussed over me. In bed for ten minutes, I'd hear a knock on the door, see her giant silhouette framed by the doorway. 'You hungry?' I ate three meals a day, plus egg sandwiches at eleven, a bowl of beans at four. I gained fifteen pounds in a month. My doctor was astounded and relieved that I was up to a normal weight. I didn't tell him that I barely ever walked, ate all day, rarely saw my children. Nat was turning me into an invalid. And I was beginning to realize that Carroll thought I'd been one all along. Hiding in the hall one night, I heard her talking to Craig in her rough whisper. 'I tell you, Nat has saved you. Saved you all.'

'It wasn't that bad, Ma,' said Craig in a cracked voice—always conciliatory, always making less of things, always talking women down.

'*Wasn't that bad?* You're like one of those frogs. If you put a frog in cold water and heat it slowly it won't notice, and before you know it—'

'You have a boiled frog. I get it.'

'Admit the house is running better.'

'Absolutely. And I thank you.'

'She needed this, Craig.'

'I know.'

'She's fragile.'

'She's been under stress, she's fine.'

They moved away at that point and I couldn't hear, but two days later, Craig started talking about therapy. God, forgive the mother of my husband.

One afternoon, with nothing else to do, I took off my dress and looked into the mirror. My hips and thighs had puffed up, thanks to Nat's forced feedings, my belly stuck out, but my arms and legs were still skinny. I looked like someone had started to blow me up, but stopped before the limbs were fully inflated. There was a dark line drawn down the centre of my torso, as if by a Chinese brush. It travelled from between my breasts, all the way to my pubis, bifurcating my belly, as if marking me for some operation. How strange pregnancy is. I still can't get over it. To house a baby inside. It makes me feel anonymous, animal. That day, as I stood in front of the mirror, I felt the most intense need to meet this baby. I suddenly had to see its face. This blankness, this image of me I saw covering up my child—I wanted to claw it away like clay. I needed to break the spell of containment, confinement; I needed to escape from Nat. I wanted to scream. And then—I swear to God it happened this way, I am not making this up—my waters broke. As I was standing there naked in front of the mirror, warm liquid travelled down my legs and gathered in a pool at my feet. Two months early. I put on some sweats and called the doctor. Left the kids with Nat. Thank God she was there, I thought, as I rushed out the door with Craig. My dear husband's face looked pinched, he avoided my gaze. He was frightened. Seven months can be enough, but not always. I knew what he was thinking. He was thinking, if we lose this baby, she won't survive.

They cut me open and lifted him out of me. After, I looked down at the ruby-red gash in my abdomen, glistening like a fleshy flower, my legs warm, numbed, itchy from anaesthesia. The doctor held the baby up. He was silent. Moving faintly. Blue. He was handed away. Three masked doctors massaged him wordlessly under orange light. I asked to hold him. No one answered. They kneaded his flesh, trying to coax his reluctant spirit back through the threshold of the world, where it hovered, undecided. Then I heard the wail, fine as a silken thread, floating through the air. I knew he would live. I knew this one was fine, just as I had known my baby sister would die from the moment I held her in my arms, though I did not know it in thoughts. She lasted two months. A child without a destiny. Sixty-one days stamped on her hand. Virginia.

The baby had to stay in the hospital for a while, and so did I. Every night, Craig came to see us, and told us how the boys were doing. Nat had shaved their heads. She said there was a head lice scare in school, but I doubted that. She had always wanted them shorn. Then there was church. She had taken them twice in one week. Craig said she even went out and bought them new, Christian-looking clothes. We laughed about it. She was living in the house. Of course she was—how else could Craig get to work by seven-thirty?

I felt so peaceful once the baby was born. I felt like I would never plan a thing again. I was cocooned in the present, all alone with baby Adam. He had to be in an incubator the first couple of days, when I wasn't breast-feeding him, but after that they let me keep him in my room. I just stared at his face for hours. The truth is, I was a little nervous about going back to real life.

But finally the day came. We drove up to the house, and I saw Kyle, my big-boned boy, walking outside with the garden hose. He had a crew cut, and was wearing a red-and-white checked shirt tucked into his jeans. He looked like something out of *Leave It to Beaver*. 'Hey!' I said. He ran to the car and looked at me shyly. He'd only been to the hospital to visit twice. He was getting used to life without me. As he peered through the back window to take a look at the baby, I wondered: *If I die, how long would he remember my face? My voice? How long till he never dreamed about me any more?* The main thing I loved about being a mother was being indispensable. The front door opened and Nat stood wearing a maroon sweatsuit, her hand on Tyler's shoulder. I got out of the car and hugged both boys.

'I hate the baby,' Tyler announced.

'Oh, now,' said Nat, 'he's your brother. He's gonna be your buddy. For now he's just a baby.' She reached in, cooing, and took Adam from the car seat, set him on her mammoth breast, where he looked as small as a ferret. I felt a mixture of envy and relief. I was so tired.

'You go up and nap,' said Nat as we walked into the sterilized kitchen. 'I'll bring him up when he starts rooting.' I climbed the stairs gratefully, the incision in my belly burning. Craig followed me. It was so amazing to be able to walk upstairs with no kids following us. Craig lay beside me and looked in my eyes. His blue-grey irises were magnified behind his round glasses. The thing about Craig is, his parents were divorced when he was eight; secretly he lives in fear that one day he'll fall out of love with me and leave, and I'll turn into a bitter and unlovable woman, like his mother. So I never know if his love is real, or if it's just distilled guilt. But I knew at that moment he loved me.

'Well, you did it again,' he said.

'I'm a little scared.'

'He's going to be fine. I'm glad Nat is here.'

'Me too. How much are you paying her, anyway?'

He shrugged. 'She's a present from my mother.'

That night, at dinner, as we were tucking into Nat's famous lasagna and chopped salad, the baby sleeping peacefully in his bassinet, a fight erupted between Kyle and Tyler. Kyle was trying to steal a cherry tomato from Tyler's plate. 'Thou shalt not covet thy neighbour's tomato,' said Craig. I stood up to wash some more. Nat shot up fast instead, chuckling. 'My husband calls me Mrs Covet,' she said, washing the tomatoes in a sieve. Craig and I looked up at her, surprised.

'I didn't know you were married, Nat,' Craig said. Nat put her hand on her hip in mock outrage.

'Whatdya think, I was an old maid? He calls me Mrs Covet 'cause whenever he orders something in a restaurant, I change my order so's I can have what he's having, 'cause it always sounds so much better than what I ordered. Mrs Covet. That's me.' From that night, Craig and I started calling Nat 'Mrs Covet' when we were alone.

Now that the baby was born I felt a little clearer in my head. And my life was so easy with Nat in charge. She had turned out to be the Mercedes of baby nurses. She kept the baby changed, bathed, in clean clothes. She gave him to me when he was about to be hungry. He was the most contented baby I had ever seen. I looked back on the other two and marvelled that I had been able to cope at all by myself. Since my sister, Virginia, died, I had been so scared that something would happen to my babies. Now, with Nat here, I felt safe. She was a nurse. She would be able to handle any emergency. I started taking better care of myself and got myself a manicure and pedicure; I had my hair blown out. I looked fat around the middle, but healthy. No one could believe I had just given birth. Craig and I went out to dinner. We made love. I started feeling better about myself, and even daydreamed about going to grad school one day.

One morning, I came upstairs and found that Nat had moved the baby's crib into her room. That way, she said, the minute he cried in the night, she could bring him in to me. It would save me getting out of bed. I thought that was a little strange. I said, 'It's okay, I don't mind getting up, I like hearing him breathe next to me.' She seemed a little put out by this, but she heaved and huffed the crib back into our room. After a few days had passed, she started saying I should think about weaning him. I had fed both the other boys myself for six months, but Nat thought that was extravagant. 'They get everything they need in the first few weeks, after that it's just comfort.'

'What's wrong with comfort?' I asked.

'This one you're not going to spoil,' she said. I thought that was an outrageous thing to say; we had a fight. She calmed me down by saying she had fallen in love with our family. She thought I was a terrific mother; my kids were the best kids she'd met aside from her own. That was the first I heard of her three children—two girls and a boy, grown now and moved away. Nat was a dark horse.

The next thing that happened was a sign, one I didn't read correctly. I was woken in the middle of the night by the sound of singing. At first I blended it into my dream. Then I opened my eyes. Adam's crib was empty. I got up and went into the hallway. The singing was coming from Nat's room. I opened the door. She was lying in her bed, Adam beside her sucking on her pinky. She blushed and muttered something about wanting to give me a few more minutes of sleep. I was furious. I took the baby back into my room, locked the door and nursed him. The next morning, Craig thought I had overreacted. 'She wanted to give you a little sleep.'

'He needs a feed in the night,' I said. 'I am his mother. I don't mind doing it. It's normal.'

'Daphne—' he looked at me, his head cocked, a pleading expression on his face.

I kept the baby with me all the next day. Nat pretended nothing had happened and she didn't try to take Adam from me. She busied herself with the other kids, cooked dinner, and then she put her coat on. We all looked at her, confused. She explained that she had to look in on her husband and tidy up her house. She would be back Monday. It was Thursday. I knew she was punishing me for what had happened the night before. Mrs Covet was letting me know that she could live without my children. The question was: *Could we live without her?* The long weekend was tough, as it turned out, but we made it. It was nice just being the family again. We ordered in pizza, watched a movie, went out to breakfast. We were sloppy. The kids got into our bed on Sunday morning and we had all three of them with us. It felt good. But when Nat appeared on Monday morning, I was glad to see her, happy to hand over the baby so I could bring the boys to school, come home and take a nap. When I got home, though, Nat's truck was gone. I walked into the house, calling her name. I went into every single room. I went to the basement, where the washing machine was. I went into the yard. My heart was racing; tears stung my eyes. The first thing I thought of was, she had to drive him to the hospital. He stopped breathing. That was what happened with Virginia.

This is how it happened: my mother brought her home in a striped blanket, a tiny woollen hat on her head, eyes shut tight, mouth pursed, fists clenched. I was five. I wanted to hold her all the time. Sometimes my mother let me give her a bottle. I loved the way she looked up at me so earnestly, her lips tugging at the rubber teet, tiny pools of milk gathering at the corners of her mouth. One afternoon, my mother had put the baby down for her nap. I had my friend Tammy over. We were pretending to be witches. We danced down the hall outside my mother's room, muttering incantations, casting spells. We spied the baby's crib and saw her little form huddled there under her striped blanket. I think I started it. I'm not sure, but I think I did. I said, 'We're going to take her away! Take her away! Take her away!' We were whispering diabolically, giggling, falling over ourselves, two witches stealing the soul of an infant. Eventually we got bored and went into the kitchen for peanut butter sandwiches and milk.

The next morning, when I woke up, the sky was still dark outside my window. I sat up and felt the cold air, took my sweater from the end of the bed and pulled it over my head. I tiptoed down the hall to my parents' room and peeked in the door. They were asleep. Virginia was in her crib; I could see her body under the blanket. I couldn't make out her face, though. It felt strange to be up before the baby; it was always her cry that woke me. It felt lonesome. I walked into the kitchen. The linoleum was frigid beneath my bare feet. I thought how proud my mother would be if I made my own breakfast. I tried to pour myself a bowl of cereal, ended up scattering cornflakes all over the table. As I was opening the refrigerator, on my toes, stretching my hand up to reach the milk, I heard my mother screaming. I ran down the hall, but my father blocked the door. 'Go to your room,' he said. I heard my mother crying out, 'I want my baby! I want my baby! I want my baby!' I went into my room and sat on my bed, held my pillow to my chest and prayed. Eventually, the ambulance came.

During the funeral, I stared at my sister's tiny, white casket, willing it to open, trying with all my might to force the lid to move even an inch. If I could kill her, perhaps I could make her live, as well. But there was no magic in me that day. I never told anyone what I had done. The guilt settled into me like a leaf falling to the ground, to be covered by other leaves and snow and earth. It melted into my being.

Nat had taken Adam to the hospital. That had to be it. I called Craig. He called the hospital. She hadn't come in. We called Nat's cell phone. It was off. Craig picked up the kids and brought them home. I called the police. Night fell. My mind turned one thought over and over, like a tumble dryer: *Mrs Covet stole my baby.*

I was up all night, though I must have drifted off at some point, because I remember dreaming about ladybugs; they were crawling all over me. I woke up thinking about bad luck. On the TV, a documentary was showing: in close-up, an Iraqi woman was tearing her hair. She was screaming, staring into the camera, her eyes almost white with fury. A blindfolded baby lay in a glass box. I didn't understand. I tuned in late. The British commentator spoke so fast. There was no medicine for her baby? Something terrible had happened to its eyes. Oh, Jesus Christ. In the desert, men in gas masks jumped off a truck. They carried machine guns. They were on their way here. All these years, without knowing, we have reached our arms around the world, dug our thumbs into that baby's eyes. We have made him blind. And now that baby's mother wanted to blind my children. She wanted to slide into their beds while they slept and breathe poison into their little pink mouths. They would wake incoherent, flailing, blind. It was my fault. I remember how smug I felt years ago when I heard the word 'sanctions' against Iraq. Such a comforting, peaceful word—like a mother's hand holding back a flailing toddler. Craig turned the TV off. I couldn't look him in the eye. It was his mother who had brought Mrs Covet into our house. His mother who hated me. Craig knew what I was thinking.

At dawn, the phone rang. They found her in Florida, picked her up in a convenience store buying pretzels. She was carrying the baby. Adam was all right. She didn't want to harm him. She just wanted him, that was all. We got on a plane with the kids and flew to Fort Lauderdale. They had the baby in the hospital there. We stayed in a hotel that night, me and Craig and the three boys. We watched the news. And there on the screen was Mrs Covet, with a serial number under her massive chin. She looked like a hardened criminal in that picture. WOMAN KIDNAPS MONTH-OLD BABY. She had no record. That's what the police said. She had been a nurse for twenty years. A married woman with three grown children, and one day she just snapped. Fell in love with our family, like she said. All that time with us, she had yearnings, she was in pain. None of us noticed. We treated her like a joke. We didn't care what was going on inside her, as long as she took care of us. Now she was in prison for kidnapping, all because she loved our baby too much. I felt bad in a way. Too much love had wrecked her life.

It's nearly light. The older children will be up soon. I cling to these moments before the day begins. I hear the baby's breathing changing; he will wake up soon. I feel the tingling pang of milk filling my breasts; a drip of it trickles down my abdomen. My third boy. He is still so new. His soft pink mouth opens, reaches out for my nipple. Eyes still shut, he roots around like a piglet. When he latches on and tastes the milk, his eyelids flutter, his eyes roll back in his head. Desire. Satiation. Desire. That's the story of his day. I am the warmth, the smell, the anchor. He is still nearly blind, innocent to meaning; he is like a pebble, a shell, a rabbit. He is no one, he is ancient, he has a face like a very old man, toothless mouth agape, staring both into and out of the void. I stay with him always. I am afraid. □

MICHAEL HAMPSON

Last Rites

The End of the
Church of England

'The best book I have
ever read about life inside
the Church of England.
Read it now before the
whole thing's gone'
Andrew Brown, *Church Times*

GRANTA BOOKS

Paperback original • £12.99
www.granta.com

FIVE HOUSES
Melanie McFadyean

PHOTOGRAPHS BY HOWARD SOOLEY

I live here, we say, this is my house, my home. We settle, dwell, adorn. A house feels permanent. But this illusion of security can end in a minute. When the illusion is shattered in childhood, as it was for me, you can spend decades harbouring a longing for that lost house, that place that seemed safe. Others, like my mother, who left her childhood home in Germany in the 1930s, somehow learn to forget. She lost her identity, her nationality, and a large fortune. In her, the shock has engendered pragmatism rather than nostalgia.

The house I lived in as a child was big, but it was nothing compared to the grandeur of my mother's. When we had to leave, we moved to grand houses, but they offered no sense of home, no safety. Then we got a small, ordinary house. I was glad to come down in the world.

This is a story of five houses: four of them I have lived in; the fifth is my mother's childhood home. The houses that we live in are significant, wrapping up the years we spend in them, making them our own. They remain when we go. To return to them is to return to a phase of your life that has passed, and to wonder which—the house or you—has changed most.

11 Cavendish Avenue, London NW8

Eleven Cavendish Avenue was—still is—a big detached house in St John's Wood, on a quiet street of similar houses, with a gravelled front garden and grey-and-white mosaic steps leading up to a porch and a large glass-panelled door. In the 1950s, everyone had net curtains: plain, expensive gauze that filtered the light and gave the rooms behind them either an atmosphere of mystery or a deadening uniformity, depending on one's mood and the weather.

I hid under a table in the sitting room on the day my father left in September 1959. He has the table still, in the house where he now lives, an antique Spanish table with curly wrought-iron supports. On top is something he calls his 'bargueno', a big varnished chest full of tiny drawers inlaid with darker wood, the kind of thing a Spanish aristocrat had his servants bear on to a galleon as he went forth to discover parts of the world that already belonged to other people. My mother has one, too.

In the 1950s, their barguenos stood side by side. When my mother was out, my older sister, Andrea, and I used to go through the drawers of her bargueno, looking for clues to the secrets we felt sure she had.

11 Cavendish Avenue, London NW8

My mother had come to England from Germany before the war. She was beautiful. She had a mysterious past we knew little about. We never went through the drawers of my dad's bargueno, because he seemed to have no mystery about him. But it turned out, eventually, that Daddy, so steady and reliable, did indeed have a secret.

In our searches we would stand on tiptoe. My mother's bargueno was large, maybe three feet high and as wide again, sitting on its own Spanish table next to my father's. We had to fiddle through tiny drawers thick with paper clips, postcards, rubber bands and thimbles, pen tops, bits of old watches, feathers, pebbles and stamps torn from envelopes—things she collected. About her we learned nothing. The letters that may have held the key to her past were in German, which we couldn't read then, and never learned later. She and her family had been driven out of Potsdam by the Nazis in the 1930s. Her mother, Daisy, lived upstairs in our house. There wasn't much toing and froing between my grandmother and my parents. There was a sense of each of us being separate.

In the autumn of 1956, after the Hungarian uprising, a young refugee called Miklos came to live with us in the basement of Cavendish Avenue. I was only five but I was alarmed on his behalf. The basement was a warren of dark rooms that included a cellar that smelled of tar and old butter and housed the boiler, a squat, blackened, susurrating thing. Beyond it was a disused kitchen where Andrea and I kept mice and a hamster which once ate her young, leaving tiny, half-gnawed pink bodies behind. I couldn't imagine anybody living there. Miklos wore a tight tweed jacket, had horn-rimmed spectacles and wavy brown hair firmly parted to one side. He taught me to roller-skate and to make tea with wiry tea-leaves. He never spoke about what had happened, or what he had seen—the Soviet tanks moved in and thousands of people died in a matter of days. He had the unsettled look of someone who is displaced—grateful and disturbed. There was no sense of any shared experience between him and my mother and grandmother, even though they were all refugees.

During the hours of daylight, my parents mostly operated as the harmonious duo they were expected to be in the 1950s, and as their children we observed their rules and rituals: no answering back, eating up greens, wonderful birthdays, bedtime stories. The outward signs were of stability and harmony: my parents had dinner parties, candlelit affairs at a large polished table. Before they went out—to return dinners, or 'drinks', or to the theatre—my mother would sit in front of her kidney-shaped dressing table with a glass top, 'putting on her face'. Once it was on she would pick up her nylons one by one from the back of a chair, roll each one down, slip a foot elegantly into the toe, and unfurl the stocking, stretching her leg out in front of her. She was slender as a mannequin and breathtakingly beautiful.

Sometimes Daisy took us up to her kitchen on the top floor, where she gave us slabs of ice-cold butter and tiny glasses of tinned fruit juice. She shared the kitchen and bathroom with Vera Bob, who came to the family as an eighteen-year-old au pair girl from the Black Forest just before I was born. Daisy had once presided over an enormous house with forty servants, but the irony of her being reduced to sharing her home with someone she probably regarded as a servant was lost on me as a child.

We loved Vera Bob deeply. She loved us as her own. She seemed to do everything—cook, make the beds, fetch us from school, look for us in summer when we were off playing until dark. Once I asked her if I could have an ice cream and she said she had no money. That an adult would be without money was a shock to me. She explained she was paid £4 a week and payday was a few days away. When we got home I stole a half-crown, a big silver coin that filled my palm, and took it upstairs to her room. I crept in. She was asleep on the bed and I was alarmed by the faint pulse beating in her neck. I put the money on her dressing table and crept out again. She never said anything to me about it; I don't think she ever mentioned it to anybody. Some forty years later I spent a night in a hospital in the Black Forest, sitting with her as she lay dying of pancreatic cancer.

Cavendish Avenue was wide and quiet and our non-school days were passed with a gang of other children, running wild, with nobody much bothering to check on our whereabouts. At weekends my dad would ride us round the garden in his wheelbarrow, and take us to the zoo. He could make the elephants do tricks—one would curtsy for the ladies and another bow for the gentleman. He had a big American car with a push-button convertible roof and once the roof had gone back, we were allowed to sit on the top of the back seat.

Although my parents showed few signs of being affected by the Beat generation, my dad was something of a dude. He played us

'Rock Around the Clock': 'When the clock strikes two/three and four/If the band slows down/we'll yell for more.' He showed us how to jive in the sitting room.

At the end of our garden, which must have been about 300 feet long and one hundred wide, was a stand of trees we nicknamed St John's Wood. It was a place to play in the way adults expect children to play, but I preferred the street. My dad made the garden beautiful with its lawn, borders, roses and raspberries, and in summer they had parties there in the evenings, with women in cocktail frocks and men in dark suits and waiters with white napkins over their arms. The men and women came in pairs: they were 'the Purbecks' or 'the Dales' or 'the Kasparis', members of a tidy, sane, safe species in standard-issue units. We watched from the house. We weren't allowed to join in.

There were things that happened in Cavendish Avenue that frightened me: the sound of shouting at night, a sudden flare of anger from an adult. I once watched from an upstairs landing as my mother rushed across the hallway below me, crying, her head in her hands. (She was wearing an ankle-length mustard-coloured robe that undulated as she moved, the sort of thing a film star would have worn.) She and my dad were having a row. Until that point I hadn't known adults cried. My mother used to sing a song sometimes, accompanying herself on the piano, which made me freeze because she looked so sad. 'He promised to buy me a bunch of blue ribbons/To tie up my bonnie brown hair./Oh dear! What can the matter be?/Oh dear! What can the matter be?/Oh dear! What can the matter be?/Johnny's so long at the fair.'

My dad used to go to America quite often. He was a lawyer with a big City firm and they had clients in Texas. One Saturday morning in the early autumn of 1959 he returned from one of these trips and Andrea and I were summoned to the sitting room. This in itself was odd, but it was also odd that he was still wearing his work suit. Only much later did I realize that maybe he had only just got home, that he hadn't been in the house the night before, that he had just come from the airport. My father and mother stood in front of the grand piano. They were standing apart, very straight. I was eight, Andrea nine. My father gave us each a parcel, something soft and bulky wrapped in brown paper with string tied in bows at the front. I was excited to get a present outside of my birthday or Christmas, but also suspicious. We unwrapped them—bright red nylon cardigans with big collars and large white plastic buttons. Rock 'n' roll cardigans, very American. Then one of my parents spoke. I don't remember which. They said that they would be getting a divorce. I thought that was something that happened in America. There was a moment's stillness, then Andrea ran screaming into the garden and hid under the trees for a long time, refusing to come out. I crept under the table with my father's bargueno on it and got in between the wrought-iron bits, trying to keep still and silent, breathing as little as possible, making myself as small as I could.

My father left immediately. Later I went up to their bedroom. He had emptied his cupboard. It smelled of Roget et Gallet carnation soap, his favourite.

After he left, my father sometimes came to see us on Saturdays. Once he took me up the M1, Britain's first new motorway, to see if his car could go a hundred miles an hour. It could. I sat in front beside him, urging him on. Most outings were similarly unsuitable. We became minor celebrities at school. In those days divorce was unusual and theirs made the news, perhaps because my father had fallen in love with Mary Malcolm, a glamorous BBC announcer. Reporters came to the door and I enjoyed talking to them until Vera Bob sent them away.

One day in the late autumn of that year I'd been roller-skating in the street on my own after school. When I came in I found Andrea and my mother sitting together in an armchair, both crying. Daisy had died. I didn't cry because I felt certain that she wasn't far away—a sense that has never left me. Not long after, Vera Bob went home to look after her mother in the Black Forest. Then we left Cavendish Avenue, having lost almost everything and everyone familiar and beloved.

Thornhill, near Stallbridge, Dorset

The following summer, in 1960, we fetched up at Thornhill. I was nine. A few weeks before, my mother had taken us to the Ritz for tea with the writer Constantine FitzGibbon. He asked us if we minded him marrying our mother. Andrea took her time replying but I was pleased because he seemed a nice man. My father had already married Mary Malcolm, and we had inherited three older stepsisters.

Thornhill was remote: a vast Palladian house set in fields, with a big wild garden of indeterminate borders. It was only recently, when I went back there, that I discovered it had been built in 1725 by Sir

James Thornhill, a painter and architect who designed the Whispering Gallery at St Paul's. When we were there, only a few rooms were furnished—Constantine's study, our bedrooms, a sitting room. The top floor had dozens of empty rooms leading off a square corridor that ran right around the house. Each room had a deep-set window with a window seat and every seat was covered in dead flies. I wandered round these rooms for hours, feeling lonely and strange. There was a huge ballroom, also empty, where I roller-skated, enjoying the sound and the rhythm of the wheels going over the wooden boards.

Thornhill's present owner has made the house look magnificent, with a Versailles-like arrangement of box hedges and a large circular fishpond by the front door. When I knocked, the door was opened by a gracious octogenarian who introduced himself as Tommy Kyle and invited me in. The ground floor was awash with light. I had forgotten the wide staircase leading up from a central hall and the glass roof that gives the space an unusual brightness. Tommy Kyle spoke with a slight American twang. He told me he had grown up in South Carolina. He took me all over the house with its astonishing wealth of old masters, antiques, enormous sofas, polished tables covered in books, flowers. The walls were deep lavender or pink. The ballroom was his bedroom, with a big four-poster with a fur cover. I asked what line of work he was in, imagining him to be an antiques dealer or an art historian. 'I move,' he said, in a mildly ironic way. 'Every seven years or so. I do up a house and I move on. This will be my last.' I congratulated him on it. 'I don't like it,' he said. Nevertheless building work was still going on. The land beyond the back windows, he said, was going to be transformed into more waterways. Versailles out front, Venice out back.

When we lived there, Constantine never did any gardening. Nor could he drive a car. Nor did he ever put on a suit and go out to work. I assumed that all men drove, went to work in a suit, came home at night, loosened their ties, got a brown drink with ice in it, smoked, told their children bedtime stories and wore rough clothes at weekends for gardening. Constantine sat in his study writing all day with a soft Venus pencil sharpened to a long point, pressing hard on a pile of foolscap paper, so that the sheets beneath bore the impression of the words above them. I wanted to draw over them to get the words to emerge, but I never dared to.

Thornhill, near Stallbridge, Dorset

I was left to my own devices much of the time. There was nobody around for miles apart from a farmer somewhere in the fields behind the house. There were no other children apart from Andrea and me. Nights at Thornhill were terrifying: the dark is so complete in the countryside it still frightens me. One night I was woken up by the commotion made by bats flying around the high ceiling. At Cavendish Avenue, if I had a nightmare, I would creep into my parents' bed or scream and my father would come to the rescue. At Thornhill, I didn't feel it was right to wake up my mother and her new husband and in any case I was too scared to go wandering around in the dark.

One wing of the house had a stone-flagged passage on the ground floor, with the kitchen and dining room off to one side and a back staircase leading down to the cellars off the other. I was walking along it to the kitchen one morning when I saw a small woman wrapped in old-fashioned brown clothes hurrying in front of me towards the glass-panelled door that led out of the house at the end of the passage. At lunchtime I asked Constantine and my mother who she was. Constantine made me describe her very carefully, then told me there was a tradition in Dorset of little spectral women dressed in brown appearing in old houses. I wasn't frightened. I felt excited and important. When I went back to Tommy Kyle's house, the flagstone passage had gone; instead there was a wide-open space, nowhere for a ghost to scuttle or melt away.

We were only at Thornhill for a matter of weeks. At the end of that summer, my sister and I were sent to boarding school. Hanford was another huge Dorset manor house, and we stood and watched as my mother disappeared down the drive, looking small in the dark green Jaguar she drove as though steering an ocean liner.

Waterston Manor, Puddletown, Dorset
While we were away at school, my mother and Constantine moved to the other side of Dorset, to Waterston Manor, which had been the model for Weatherbury, Bathsheba Everdene's house in Thomas Hardy's *Far from the Madding Crowd*. This was to be home for four years but it never felt like it. Andrea and I spent more time at boarding school than anywhere else. Holidays were split between parents; my father lived in London. I don't suppose we were ever at Waterston for more than three weeks at a time. Though not as big

as Thornhill, it was enormous by most people's standards, and big enough to be divided, so that Andrea and I slept in the relatively new addition some distance from the rest of the family. In 1961, my mother had my brother, Francis.

The main house had been partly destroyed by a fire in 1863. Two sides had survived: one, the rear façade, included three alcoves with statues in them that framed Francis's bedroom window; the other faced east and was Jacobean. The garden ran to acres. Great stretches of lawn were divided by a fishpond running up the middle and flanked by a sunken garden with irises and Chinese maples on one side and exotic bamboo woodland on the other. There were greenhouses, thousands of daffodils along the river in spring, a walled kitchen garden, a gravel drive, stables with a yard and attached to it a cottage where I wished we lived. The whole thing was very pretty, really, but neither the house nor the beautiful surroundings alleviated the sense that it was supposed to be home and just wasn't.

To one side of the lawn was a catalpa tree under which on sunny days Constantine had tea. Constantine was a novelist and a historian. During the war he had been an intelligence officer with the American army in Germany, and some of his research was used at the Nuremberg trials. Afterwards he wrote a book about German resistance to Hitler. He was famously a friend of Dylan Thomas, whose biography he was writing at Waterston. When he married my mother, he'd just had a great success with his novel *When the Kissing Had to Stop*.

Constantine was a man of habit, always had tea at the same time, usually a sandwich filled with something he called 'Cad's Paste'— Patum Peperium, fishy stuff from Fortnum & Mason's—and a slice of fruit cake. His working routine involved hours writing in an oak-panelled room or in the summer-house, while my mother took up market gardening. She had a handsome young man to help her, Mick, whose tight jeans and narrowed eyes were secretly noticeable to me as a bored eleven year old.

We had lunch with the adults but never dinner. Lunch was always in the dining room with its silver-embossed wallpaper, gleaming table and views across the lawn to a copper beech tree. We were expected to display good manners and make intelligent conversation, very unlike my father's noisy, crowded kitchen table round which we sat with our stepsisters. Dinner at Waterston, on the other hand, was fun: we had it in the small tatty sewing room with Francis's nanny, a comfy middle-aged woman of deliberate plainness. We'd have our plates on our knees and watch a small black-and-white television. We watched *I Love Lucy*, *Dr Finlay's Casebook*, *Steptoe and Son*, *Rawhide*, *The Two Ronnies*, *Sunday Night at the London Palladium*. After each advertisement, Nanny always said with a chuckle and a wink, 'I'll have one of those then.' She also told jokes. 'What did the bra say to the top hat? You go on ahead and I'll give these two a lift.'

Lunch often involved guests, especially at weekends. One of the regulars was Arthur Koestler, who came with his partner, Cynthia, a pale, terrified woman who never spoke. Koestler had a low guttural voice and looked to me like a cross between a crocodile and a wolf. He seemed to absorb all the oxygen, all the vitality in the room, so whether he was speaking or silent we were dragged into his doomy forcefield. Constantine, on the other hand, would sometimes laugh so much he had to mop his face with a spotty handkerchief, which alarmed me. I'd never seen anyone laugh like that. I look back on it with admiration. There's something indomitable about people who laugh at their own jokes even if nobody else does.

We rarely said anything unless called upon to do so. Among the other guests was Tony Crosland, the Labour MP, and his American wife, Susan, who was very glamorous and had pink hair like candy floss, and Colin Welch, the deputy editor of the *Daily Telegraph*, and his wife, Sybil, who were attractively eccentric. Colin would arrive on a motorbike dressed in black leather, cracking risky jokes in his panthery voice. Henry Moore, the sculptor, was a friend of Constantine's and my brother's godfather. There was great excitement when he was said to be sending a 'maquette' as a late wedding present. I thought a maquette was a macaque. I didn't like to ask why their friend was sending them a monkey. When it transpired that there was to be no macaque, I was disappointed. I had quite wanted to see how Constantine and my mother would cope with a monkey. Having learned a maquette was some kind of statue, I imagined it would be something pretty you could put in the garden, perhaps a cupid with an arrow or a dolphin spouting water from its lips. When it arrived, my mother and stepfather cut open the box in awed wonder. For all its size and fanfare it held a small thing that looked like an ashtray.

I liked Henry Moore. He played drawing games with us on rainy

Waterston Manor, Puddletown, Dorset

afternoons by the end of which the floor would be knee-deep in drawings which he made us do with our eyes closed. He did them, too.

Every day before lunch my mother would drive Constantine to one of the pubs he frequented. The nearest villages were called Puddletown, Piddlehinton and Piddletrenthide. I went with her to collect him one day from an ancient pub in Piddlehinton called the European, which is still there. I remember it was low, beamy and dark, with a few old men muttering companionably in the gloom. The barman let me pull the pints and the old men were telling Constantine about the pints they had shared with Thomas Hardy, who died in 1928, when they would have been in their thirties and forties.

Despite its array of intellectual weekend guests, Waterston seemed cut off from the rest of the world. Probably the adults talked about world events at lunchtime, but like most children I had little interest in such things. So when my mother started stockpiling tins of food in 1962 in something she called the 'Cuba cupboard', I had no idea that this was her response to an international crisis.

It was at Waterston, in 1963, that I was by the front door on my way out when the phone rang in the cloakroom attached to the hallway. It had a loud clanging ring. Constantine answered it. I paused to listen. He didn't see me. 'Louis dead?' he said. I can still hear the quiet, shocked tone of his voice forty years later. There would be phone calls like that for me as I got older, people I was close to. 'Robin dead? Dave dead? Ian dead? Paul dead? Lucy dead?' And in those phone calls, the same sense of absurdity and grief at the transience of it all. That day it was Louis MacNeice who had died.

I went back to Waterston this summer. I walked along beside the fishpond with its lilies and goldfish, flanked by weathered flagstones. with lime-green *Alchemilla mollis* flowers between the cracks. At the back of the garden is a spinney dominated by a huge copper beech tree. I stood underneath it. I used to do that when we lived there. Adam Tyndall, the owner, has been there for thirty years and brought up four children in the house, but now, with his children grown up, he is selling it. He is a widower and lives with a widow, a former neighbour. The house is 300 years old. A part of the copper beech was blown down by the 1987 hurricane. Adam Tyndall counted the rings on the fallen timber, 150 rings, each denoting a year.

13 Mortimer Crescent, London NW6

After four years in Dorset, my mother's marriage to Constantine collapsed and she moved back to London. Nobody seemed to notice that my scattered sense of home was making me ever wilder. Just after we left Waterston, I was expelled from Sherborne School for Girls after a year. I joined Andrea at Cranborne Chase in Wiltshire, such a degenerate and lawless place that I had to go in search of the rules in order to break them. It took me two and a half years to get expelled.

The expulsion came with no warning. I rang my father one Sunday and could tell something was wrong. He said he was meeting me off a train that afternoon. I confronted the headmistress moments later, just as she was giving the spiel to prospective parents clutching tiny glasses of sherry. Shielding the parents with her body as if from a serious menace, she murmured to them meaningfully, 'Broken home', then ushered them out protectively, with some excuse to me about having to expel me for the good of the school.

My mother by then had moved into a house in what Andrea and I called Kilburn and our mother called West Hampstead. We had, to my delight, come down in the world. Thirteen Mortimer Crescent was a decrepit, end-of-terrace Victorian house. It had charm. It was welcoming. It was smaller than anywhere else we had lived. It looked out on to a hideous block of flats in front and a building site at the back. It shook as diggers and tractors lumbered about in the mud behind our garden wall. I had the smallest room. It was my choice. I felt safe in it.

My mother had no money or earning power to speak of, although she has many talents and had always worked——at art restoration, illustration, translation, garden design. But she had just been given a cheque from the West German government, which had begun to pay out war reparations in compensation for the loss of her family's house before the war. She made no drama out of this: it was a useful cheque, end of story. It paid for 13 Mortimer Crescent.

At Mortimer Crescent, for the first time in our lives, we were free of the subliminal tension created by strained marital relations. My mother was a little tragic at the start, but she soon had a collection of admirers who sought to please us as a way of getting to her heart. And for the first time since Cavendish Avenue, a house came close to providing a home. I felt I belonged there. Its doors didn't hang straight, bits of it were always falling off, but that didn't matter. The things my mother carried with her from house to house—her bargueno, the few paintings that had survived from her childhood home, the antiques she had bought for a few shillings before collecting junk was fashionable—these found their place as, perhaps ironically, did she. She was as far from her childhood glories as she had ever been. Life was a struggle for her materially, but she was happier and more easygoing, more herself, in that house than in the ones that had gone before; their architecture, history and grandeur promising much and delivering little. This was the only house that we lived in where nothing terrible happened. Nobody close to us died while we lived there, nobody left us. Andrea and I did our last bit of growing up in it. She left school and became an art student, fell in love with a fellow student and left home to get married at eighteen. I left there to go to university. When my mother sold the house she, too, was to be married, for the third time. She had met a charming, handsome man she called John 'Paradiso', whose surname was really Whitehorn. John told me to follow my secret heart and then went ahead and followed his by divorcing his wife and marrying my mother. It was a very happy marriage.

I spent a last magical summer there alone. I was eighteen and revelling in a sense of freedom from the past and the promise of the future. It was 1969. I had friends to stay and marijuana to smoke.

Thirteen Mortimer Crescent was the last house we lived in together. I went to university in Leeds, Andrea and her new husband went to America, my mother and John with my brother, Francis, moved to a house in St John's Wood only seconds from my father's house. On John and my mother's wedding day, I visited my father. We sat in his garden. I asked him if he could hear voices and clinking glasses nearby. It was the sound of my mother's wedding party in her new back garden, about three gardens away from his. They never talked to one another. Even if they met by chance in the local high street the lengthiest exchange was a curt hello. It wasn't until Andrea was dying of cancer in April 1983 that they spoke to one another again. We were at St Thomas's Hospital the morning she died, in a small rooftop garden. They hovered beside a tub full of plants, desolately weeding it and speaking to each other haltingly and quietly. He took her home after Andrea died.

Thirteen Mortimer Crescent was demolished soon after we left in 1969 and a small faceless block of flats was built on its site.

Herbertshof, Bertinistrasse, Potsdam, Berlin

It was years before I felt any real interest in my mother's childhood home. I had seen a few photographs of Herbertshof in its heyday and equated its style and opulence with the privileges and exclusivity that enormous wealth brings. I wasn't comfortable with that. I dislike stately homes. I had a problem with the idea of forty servants. This reaction, a mixture of discomfort and amused scorn, distanced me from wanting to know the whole story. I thought I knew enough. I thought that my grandparents had been lucky to escape with their lives. Millions weren't, among them my grandfather's brother Fritz, who died in Theresienstadt, and his wife, Louise, who was gassed in Auschwitz. It wasn't until 1994, when I was already in my forties, that I went to the house in Potsdam for the first time, and even then it was more or less by accident.

In 1990, the new united German government had restituted the house to my mother and her brothers. I happened to be in Berlin for work, and I thought I might as well go to Potsdam and have a look. Herbertshof is one of several huge houses on Bertinistrasse, a sandy track running beside a lake, the Jungfernsee. I might easily have walked past it. The house was partially hidden behind a high wooden barricade topped with barbed wire. The yellow stucco had fallen off long ago. Most of the windows were broken. A searchlight was perched on the edge of a crumbling first-floor balcony. One of its inhabitants, a gang of some sixty squatters, had painted *Trots all dem*—'In spite of them all'—in black Germanic lettering over the gateway in front of which my grandmother Daisy once posed for a photograph in a big Mexican hat. In the photo you can see part of the word Herbertshof spelled out in wrought-iron lettering on the wall behind her. The letters were still there. I knocked on the door. A young North African woman, one of the squatters, opened the door a crack and looked at me suspiciously. I said I was researching the history of the house and could I come in? I was sure the squatters, threatened with eviction by the local council, wouldn't let me in knew if they knew my connection to the house. She shook her head and shut the door.

I went down to the lake and wandered past the dilapidated

remains of the border wall that had marked East from West until five years before. There were swastikas among the neon graffiti. Barges heaved by on the water. I struck up a conversation with a skinny, peroxide-haired punk with heavy eyes who was on his way back to Herbertshof. He told me the house belonged to a rich Jewish banker whose family wouldn't be getting it back. Why should they? Hitler, he said, let the Jews take everything with them when they left.

After that visit I began to ask questions about Herbertshof, my mother and her family's past. I asked her about her childhood and I looked through the boxes of papers relating to her family and the story of the house that were stored in my cousin's attic. In those boxes I found a collection of sepia photographs of Herbertshof that I had never seen before. They were taken in 1921, the year my mother was born. These are professional photographs taken to show off the house, its ornate exterior and one after another of its softly lit, heavily furnished rooms; a portrait of the house as a symbol of solidity and respectability, luxury and ease; an expression of Herbert's sense of his place in the world.

My grandfather Herbert Gutmann bought the house in 1913 and named it after himself. My mother spent her childhood dodging her English governess, roaming the gardens and woods, swimming in the lake in summer, skating on it in winter. Her parents were social figures in Weimar Berlin, famous for their hospitality. I found my grandmother Daisy's diaries, written in red exercise books, that testify to the life they led: dinners and garden parties for 200, visits from kings, trips to London, Paris and Bucharest, tea with the Reichspresident, Hindenburg. My mother still has the visitors' book from Herbertshof, its list of names surprisingly eclectic: Harold Nicolson and Vita Sackville-West, the painter Max Liebermann, the theatre director Max Reinhardt, who was Jewish and emigrated in 1934, as did the psychoanalyst Vera von der Heydt. Some of the visitors later became Hitler's henchmen, such as Hjalmar Schacht, his economics minister, and Joachim von Ribbentrop, his foreign minister. And also there are Andrew and Dora McFadyean, my father's parents, who lived in Berlin in the 1920s because my grandfather was on the Reparations Committee set up after the First World War. My father lived in Berlin for some of his childhood, but he didn't visit the house or meet my mother until 1940.

Herbertshof, Bertinistrasse, Potsdam, Berlin

In her diaries Daisy notes that 1931 was 'the last carefree year' but she hardly refers to its key event—Herbert's resignation from his post as director of the Dresdner Bank. On the weekend of July 11–12 there was a major financial crisis in Germany and, for reasons that are still not clear, Herbert was forced to resign. In his memoirs my uncle Luca, my mother's brother, wrote that his father returned on the Sunday night, after being at crisis meetings all weekend, and said that he had 'young Turk' enemies within the bank and that the government was looking for scapegoats to appease the wild men on the extreme political right. 'They had to throw something to the wolves.' Later there were posters that, my uncle said, showed 'a vicious caricature of our father, side by side with a former Socialist Party leader'. The caption read: 'These two parasites conspire to destroy the true Germany.'

Herbert didn't think of himself as Jewish. His father, Eugen Gutmann, who had founded the bank in 1872, had converted to Protestantism after being warned by Bismarck that if he didn't, his career would not progress. Herbert saw himself as a good German and a good Protestant, a man of influence who moved the money and held the centre. After his forced resignation, he was demoted to an insignificant role in the bank with a small income. He still had some fifty directorships and a massive art collection, but as Daisy wrote in September 1932, 'The heydays [were] ending. Friends and acquaintances still come out but no longer in huge numbers.' It was about this time that my mother discovered that she was part-Jewish, classified by the Nazis as a *mischlinge grade eins*, a mixture grade one—Jewish on her father's side, gentile on her mother's.

In September 1933 they moved out of the house. Daisy noted briefly, 'Herbertshof became too expensive to run...because of the bank row.' They locked it up and rented one nearby. Villa Alexander was smaller but still pretty grand. 'We had to let the servants go,' Daisy wrote. 'I found it difficult...compared with the glamorous beautiful harmonious days of the past but we made the best of it...the children were happy...nice to enjoy the peace lying in the sun...under the great plane trees and the tulip tree.'

Nine months later, on Saturday June 30 1934, my mother was coming home along Bertinistrasse when she saw her father being arrested and taken away. This was the weekend of the Night of the

Long Knives, when Hitler settled his scores with dissenting members of the SA, the Brownshirts who had brought him to power, and others against whom he bore grudges. Hundreds were killed. There is no reliable record of why Herbert was either arrested or spared, but it's likely that the arrest was connected to his friendship with Kurt von Schleicher, who was murdered with his wife in the early hours of that morning. Daisy and Herbert were expecting them to lunch. After the murder, Hitler accused von Schleicher, who had briefly been Chancellor in 1932, of plotting against him.

My mother's brother Fred, who died two years ago, made a spectacular addition to these events which is impossible to corroborate. When I wrote to him, asking what he thought happened that weekend, he wrote back saying that von Schleicher had hired Herbert's chauffeur to assassinate Hitler in 1934. There is no record of any such attempt. Fred continued: 'A day or two after the attempt the Gestapo turned up at our house. They arrested Papa as a possible accomplice. After a bribe, an armed SS man told us their destination was the Oranienburg concentration camp.' But Herbert was returned to the house by the SS later that night, along with two of his friends, one of them Konrad Adenauer, who became the first West German Chancellor after the war. The jails and police cells were full and so they were to be held under house arrest. For about a week nobody was allowed in or out. Fred's story continues: 'Apparently Papa had indirectly approached Göring through a Nazi sympathizer and friend, Eddy von Gontard...and offered Göring any painting in exchange for his and two of his fellow prisoners' freedom.' There was a more plausible rumour about why Herbert was spared: that his brother-in-law, the Italian ambassador to Germany, used his influence to free him. Whatever the reason, my grandfather came home.

After this Daisy wrote: 'People don't want to see us because they're frightened for their position and of being spied on. They avoid me because my family is not Aryan.' But despite the dangers, Herbert and Daisy didn't leave Berlin until October 1936, by which time Daisy was terrified: 'We felt imprisoned. I was frightened.' In October 1936: 'There came as if from heaven an invitation to a meeting in Basel which was approved by Hjalmar Schacht. The whole point is to get to the border.' They didn't want it to seem that they were leaving for good, as there were laws designed to strip emigrating Jews of their wealth and attempts to spirit out money could result in the death penalty. Herbert would be a prime target. He and Daisy needed the right paperwork to ease their passage out of the country and to make it look as if they had every intention of returning—which perhaps they did.

Once they had exit papers signed by Schacht (who had once worked at my grandfather's bank before throwing in his lot with the Nazis and agreeing to raise money for Hitler), they could leave without arousing suspicion.

But before they left Berlin, they went back to Herbertshof: 'Herbert's last day. So much unknown before us, but goodbye to the terror, goodbye to the home where his children were so happy. When we crossed the Swiss border at Basel, we had tears in our eyes after the dreadful tension and the new feeling of freedom.' Daisy and Herbert went on to Italy to stay with his sister. There they received a postcard from a friend telling them the weather was bad in Germany and they shouldn't return, implying that it was too dangerous. They went to England, where they had many friends. Luca was already in London. Fred had managed to get to the United States. My mother was left behind at the Villa Alexander for another year. She says she felt no sense of being abandoned. She says it would have looked suspicious if they had all left at the same time, and her parents wanted her to complete her education. 'With hindsight,' she told me, 'you can see the dangers, but I wasn't frightened. I thought, like the adults, that it was a passing thing, Hitler was ridiculous, it wouldn't work. We knew there were concentration camps but we had no real idea. Many friends left and told Papa we should go, but Papa was an optimist and he didn't want to believe anything ghastly could happen.'

She stayed at the villa with their housekeeper, Barbl Schmidt. The winter of 1936–7 was a bad one and when their money ran out Barbl sold furniture to buy food and coal. My mother used to go at dawn to Herbertshof, a few minutes' walk away, to take vegetables that had been stored below ground from the kitchen gardens. The head gardener had taken over and she was too frightened to ask for them.

In October 1937 her mother came back to get her. The visit didn't go unnoticed, as Luca wrote in his memoirs: 'The Gestapo rang [the Villa Alexander] one night to enquire whether her husband had "shifted his millions abroad".' Daisy told my mother that if anyone asked she should say that they had invitations to go on holiday to England. They left by boat from Bremerhaven on October 9, with a few marks and a suitcase each. The boat was bound for New York and stopped at Southampton.

Two years later Herbertshof was sold for a knockdown price under a forced sale to a Nazi front organization called Volksbund fur Deutschtum im Ausland. The money was put into a blocked account. Herbert got nothing. By then most of his money had been taken in the 'fleeing tax' levied by the Nazis on Jews leaving Germany. He filled in forms in 1937, 1938 and 1939, sent to him in exile, copies of which I found in the boxes in my cousin's attic. They were demands for taxes, all of which, having secured a loan, Herbert paid. One was 'for the atonement of being Jewish', another for 'Sühneopfer'—expiatory sacrifice. The Gestapo wrote to him in November 1939 revoking his German citizenship. The British interned Luca in a Canadian internment camp, where he received his last letter from Herbert. 'Don't worry about me,' Herbert wrote, ' I have had a wonderful, fulfilling life. You should always be happy and sing the song of life.' He died on December 22 1942, aged sixty-three, in a little house in Paignton, Devon, where they were living. 'He fell asleep peacefully in my arms,' Daisy wrote. 'A rich and kind life was finished, too noble for this fickle world. Now there were only shadows around me...'

It would be another sixty years before any of his family set foot in the house again. My mother and her brothers, having had it restituted to them, decided to pass it on to their children—my brother, myself, and our three cousins. In 2000 I went back to Herbertshof, this time with my cousin Nick, Luca's son, and his wife, Judy. With us was an official from the Deutsche Stiftung Denkmalschutz, the German National Trust, and a journalist from the *Frankfurter Allgemeine Zeitung*. I hadn't realized how much there had been about the 'Gutmann Villa' in the press.

The way into the house was through the garden door leading off a patio. In the photographs I'd found, this patio was a lovely secluded place sheltered by walls covered in a rambling rose. Now it was a dump for anything the squatters had thrown out. I hung back as the others went in, noting the obligatory supermarket trolley, a gutted television, ragged bits of clothing, discarded mechanical tools, bits of old vehicles, tangled grass, nettles, brambles and dock. I rang my mother on my mobile, telling her where I was. She sounded shocked. She asked me to describe what I could see. I told her and she sighed. She didn't ask about anything else.

I went into the house on my own. The cold was damp and raw and chilled me to the bone. Broken glass and rubble crunched underfoot. The windows were still boarded up and let in barely any light, just enough to see the paint peeling off the walls.

I could hear the voices of the others upstairs. I paused to get my bearings, trying by the light of a torch to match what I could see with what I had seen in the photographs. But at some point—perhaps during the war, when the house had been a Wehrmacht hospital, or after it, when it was a children's clinic, or in the time of the GDR, when it was an old people's home—the ground floor had been carved up into a catacomb of small dark chambers The squatters had used these bunkers for vehicle maintenance. Only the ballroom had been left untouched, though it was dirty and done-in, with a canoe sitting in the middle of the floor and a banner strung above it that read *Herzliche Wilkommen*—'You are very welcome'.

The upstairs rooms were in such savage disarray it looked as if their inhabitants had suddenly fled in terror. There was no need for torches here; enough light found its way through the security screens on the windows. The floors were ankle-deep in discarded possessions, clothes and books everywhere. The police had evicted the squatters early one morning six months earlier, after which the house had been boarded up and an alarm system installed.

Despite all the debris, I found Daisy's boudoir, which was next to her and Herbert's bedroom. Perhaps it was here she wrote her diary and pressed the flowers I found in them, fragile and faded, with that musty scent of petals. I could imagine her dressed in pale-blue chiffon or silk to match her eyes, the same colour as my mother's, her dark hair gathered up, writing, in August 1931: 'Tea today with the Maharani of Baroda... We had a detective in the entrance hall by the guest book when Lord Birkenhead came to stay. He shocked the butler by asking for beer before breakfast.' In September they went to London to lend her Persian earrings to the Royal Academy for an exhibition. They ate oysters, went to the theatre, 'I met Rabindranath Tagore again...then to the House of Lords after lunch at the

Savoy...Claridges...Quaglinos...fun in the Café Anglais...I danced.'
Three years later, looking back she writes, 'The elegant life continued
and we stayed in the Crillon in Paris, very poche [*sic*]. I really revelled
in the wonderful life and today I'm glad I did.'

The old photograph of her boudoir shows an exotic mix of
styles—a patterned tiled floor, Turkish rugs, a deep floral-covered
sofa, a chandelier, a dressing table complete with mirror and glass
jars, a roll-top desk with an inkstand and pen, a corner table covered
with framed photographs, vases of flowers dotted around. On the
window sill I found a letter written by a squatter. One line read: 'I
want to stay here but I have to leave my little paradise and it's
fucking hard to do it.'

At the end of a maze of corridors I found myself on a narrow back
staircase, which led to a small space like a den with a latticework
front. I peered through the lattice and down below I could see the
Arabicum—the Arabian room Herbert had bought in Syria and had
transported back to Germany and installed at Herbertshof in a wing
built specially for it. It looked much as it had at the time the
photographs were taken. Narrow beams of sunlight penetrated the
gaps in the screens covering the tall windows, catching the dust and
illuminating the spacious room with its dark hand-painted wooden
panelling and mirrors stained with mercury. A pale, fragile ostrich egg
with a feather attached to its base, familiar from the photographs,
was hanging from the ceiling. It had survived everything.

My mother used to hide in this little space. She called it the harem.
From there, eye-level with the ostrich egg, she would look down and
listen to her father and his friends talking, often, she says, about
Lenin and the Bolsheviks.

We sold Herbertshof in the winter of 2005 for a fraction of its
potential value, a lot less than my terraced house in north
London is worth. I didn't mind. Profit wasn't the point. I had got
something much more than money out of the house.

The sale attracted media attention partly because one of the new
owners is a famous German actress, Nadia Uhl. When I asked another
of its new owners, Olaf Elias, an antiques' salvage expert, why he
thought the house had attracted so much media coverage, he said it
was because it represented what Germans felt about their past. It

elicits emotional responses, he said, not all of them comfortable or easy to articulate.

It is almost seventy years since my mother left Herbertshof and she has never been back. She says she wants to remember it as it was. She is a pragmatist. In the aftermath of adversity, she shrugs or chuckles and she is not sentimental. Perhaps that coolness is a defence against revisiting the sense of loss I imagine she experienced as a child. Perhaps not. I think she dispensed with the past a long time ago.

The houses I have lived in stay with me. I return to them in dreams, but they are never quite right. They lose their correct definitions. One spring afternoon not long ago I happened to be in St John's Wood and drove down Cavendish Avenue, as quiet as it was in the 1950s and little changed. A woman was standing at the gate of number eleven. I stopped and asked if I could go in. She was the caretaker, nobody was living there, and she said she would take me in. None of the empty rooms were as they had been. I couldn't find a room I recognized on the ground floor or the upper floors. Where there had been that labyrinthine basement, there was open space full of light. The garden had been landscaped beyond recognition. I felt momentarily angry and then, once I had left, released. The sense of home which I had always felt eluded me, the longing for that lost house, had gone. □

EARLY RETIREMENT
John Lanchester

Bill Lanchester, circa 1968

My father used to tell the story of a tutor at his university, a Viennese professor of something or other. There was a general conversation about what people would have, if they could have anything in the world. There were some surprising answers—a youngish woman don said she wanted an enormous wine cellar. When it came to the old Viennese, he sucked his pipe for a moment, and then said, 'Vell, if I could really have anything I wanted, anything at all, I think I would choose... *permanent* delusions of grandeur.'

Dad loved that story. He liked it because it was funny, but I also think he liked the idea of a permanent state of feeling that excluded difficulty or pain. For instance, he could never bring himself to discuss money. He could talk about it in the abstract, in relation to businesses in the news or tax policy. But he couldn't bear to talk about money in any personal context to do with his income or—and this was a particular issue—my pocket money. I wasn't allowed to ask for money or even to mention it. The subject caused Dad too much pain. It touched on things from his own childhood to do with the fact that his father had used money as a means of control and interference.

What was odd about this was that my father worked for a bank. Dealing with money was what he did all day, every day, for his entire working life. And yet he couldn't bear to speak of it at home. As a teenager I would resort to simply stealing money from his wallet rather than having to put him and me through the impossible ordeal of asking for it. I would steal it resentfully, too, from the wallet he left lying on the hall table, as if giving me permission to steal from it. I felt that I didn't want to steal but had no choice, and that the whole episode was showing both our characters in their least good light. I now see that the banking and the not-being-able-to-discuss-money were tightly linked: he had gone to work in a bank because his father had bullied him into doing a job which would keep him grounded in the real world—which, in his father's world-view, meant doing a job which was all about money. The memory of that, and all that it implied, was so painful for Dad that if I ever mentioned money to him, he was overpowered by flashbacks from his youth and sent into a gloom.

We lived in Hong Kong, where my father was working, first as deputy and then as manager, at the North Point branch of the Hongkong and Shanghai Bank. He must have felt that his best years in career terms were in front of him: he was serving a long apprenticeship as a relative junior, but that wasn't unusual for the bank in its colonial days. He would still have expected to start to rise and for big opportunities to open up. That might seem like a naïve hope for someone who had already spent seventeen years working for the same company; but the pace of banking life, like that of other forms of work, was slower in those days. His chance might yet come.

When it did, in the late 1960s, it was in the form of a transfer to head office in Hong Kong: the bank's HQ at 1 Queen's Road Central. Today, that address is occupied by a famous building designed by Norman Foster—at the time it was built, the most expensive privately owned building in the world, and a highly ugly and impractical one too. In those days the bank was a chunky stone structure with a lovely central hall illustrated with a mural of striving workers; it was so low, relative to the Hong Kong of my childhood, that it was impossible to believe that when my grandparents were first in Hong Kong it was the tallest building in the city. This was where my father was to spend the rest of his working life. It's where I best remember him as a working man, when I used to drop in on him, semi-unannounced. I would either ring up to his secretary from the banking floor, or simply sneak into the staff lift and go up to his section before asking to be taken in by the 'boy'—a Cantonese man in his forties who was this section's administrative manager. Dad was always pleased to see me and I him, and there was something very reassuring about my father in his office in his shirtsleeves at the centre of all this bustle, a picture of me and my mother on his desk.

In his career, though, my father was a disappointed man. He climbed to the stair below the top one, in terms of the bank's hierarchy. He was a senior member of the overseas staff, well paid and as secure as any worker in the world, the beneficiary of a pension scheme which, as it happened, he helped design. But the next level up was that of the head honchos, the people who decided things and set the course, as opposed to running things and keeping them on course. He never got to that level. He had a platform with a perfect view of the personalities and political issues at the high levels of the bank, and he worked with three men who were eventually to run the organization, and oversee the process which took it from being a minor colonial bank to one of the biggest financial institutions in the world. One thing he told me I often remember: two of the chairmen he had known were, he said, diametrically opposite in their behaviour to colleagues. One would scream and shout and berate them, but he never sacked anybody. The other was mild-mannered and calm and never raised his voice, but was utterly ruthless and would sack and demote people without hesitation. I've kept that in mind ever since, and it's been borne out: in every organization I've ever seen at close range, the bosses tend to be either screamers or sackers. People have either a bark or a bite, almost never both.

The next level of promotion, however, did not come. There were one or two attempts by other senior bank figures to poach him to go and work for them—once, by a friend of my father's who was setting up a merchant bank to wheel and deal, in what was to be the far more buccaneering style of banking so prevalent in the 1980s and since. But my father's superior fought off the move, mainly, it seems, because he needed Dad to do all the work and run the department. My father saw this as a disappointment, and so it was, since the main thing in life isn't so much what happens to us as what we think happens to us. I do wonder, though. The cure for being a banker wasn't to be a more interesting kind of banker; it was, probably, not to be a banker at all. But it's hard to accept, once you have been doing a thing for so long, that you have been doing the wrong thing.

Duty was important for him. He was a good man, in his unostentatious and shy way one of the best men I have known. He grew up in a culture in which duty and reticence and honour and privacy and lack of ostentation were all regarded as forms of goodness and public-spiritedness. Plenty of people still believe in all these things, but they have vanished from our public culture, or at least from our publicized culture, and no one celebrates them any more, or even admits that they were once seen, and not so long ago, as virtues. One aspect of this was the good deeds he did, and another was that he never spoke about them. I knew that he was appointed to sit on the Hong Kong rent tribunal, overseeing arguments between landlords and tenants—a highly sensitive position in a place where there is no freehold land, and a tribute to his reputation for fair-mindedness. It was also a tribute to the fact that he had taken the time to go to night classes and learn functional Cantonese, something few expatriates bothered to do, not least because it is so difficult. But there were things

I did not know. In our latter years in Hong Kong, from the early 1970s onwards, we came to know a group of Catholic nuns who were lively and funny and did a variety of demanding jobs, mostly linked to poverty relief—one was a surgeon, another the private secretary to Cardinal Wu; others we met later were involved in medical aid work in Guangzhou. They had the unusual virtue in Hong Kong of being equal-opportunity sceptics, as unillusioned about the Communist Chinese as about Britain and the self-serving billionaires and big shots of the Hong Kong business community. I had always assumed that we met them through my mother's Irish contacts in what my father always called 'the Murphia'. Much later I found out that we knew them because my father served unpaid as the treasurer of one of the local hospitals, where some of the nuns worked. I had had no idea: he never mentioned it in front of me. That is how you are supposed to do charity, with the left hand not knowing what the right is doing, and it is the best side of my father's reticence.

My awareness of my father's unhappiness at work was not a vivid thing. He did not complain at length, only in muted asides. He felt that he was brighter and more able than the people he worked for. As for his work, he hardly every spoke about it, and only once showed me papers he had brought home when there was a choice between three candidates applying for a senior job. He spread out the papers, explained who the men were, and then said that although one of them was obviously the best and brightest he wouldn't get the job because he was too spiky and cocky and wouldn't necessarily fit in. That, he explained, is how things often worked. People want to have a quiet time and don't like to be disrupted, even if it is by someone who in other ways is the best man for the job.

The defining event of all these years happened in 1974, when my father had a serious heart attack while in the office. Until this point he had, in twenty-five years of employment, not missed a single day's work through illness, something of which he was very proud, especially because he had so often been sickly in his childhood. He was forty-seven years old and a smoker, getting through a pack of Benson & Hedges Gold a day, but apart from being overweight—not obese, but overweight—and sedentary there were no warnings. Years afterwards he told me two things about his heart attack. One was that the first symptoms were like those of indigestion. At the time

I didn't understand what a glimpse this was into a world of constant, tormenting anxiety. He also told me that at the moment of having the heart attack he felt himself falling over, losing his footing as he collapsed, so that whenever now he began to lose his balance, on something like a carpet that was slipping over a smooth floor underneath, he had a flashback to the moment of losing consciousness during the heart attack. Again, I didn't understand how terrible the ensuing anxiety and sense of apprehension must have been. The main thing I saw was the physical caution which never left my father afterwards, and the regular angina attacks he used to suffer when out walking, which would cause him to pause and catch his breath with his fists resting on his hips—a syndrome called 'window shopper's angina'. He kept his nitroglycerine pills on him at all times, and latterly we had an oxygen cabinet in the coat cupboard. He gave up smoking, began to take regular exercise in the form of walking, and never ate so much as a mouthful of butter or bacon again.

My father had had difficulties with phobias and anxieties in the past. Wide open spaces triggered moments of irrational fear, and so did moving from dark places into sunlight suddenly; he once said to me he thought the feeling might be linked to traumatic hidden memories about being born. He dreaded social situations that he couldn't get out of, and had a particular fear of restaurants; he would have to walk up and down outside them for a while, summoning the nerve to go in. These anxieties were taken to a different level by the heart attack, since he now had reason to worry that he might overtax his heart by panicking and suffer another infarct. In other words, the anxiety gave him a powerful legitimate reason to feel more anxious.

I don't want to make my father's life sound unrelievedly grim. He was a popular colleague and people were quick to like him: he was unpompous in a time and a place when that wasn't a common trait in men. He was gentle, funny, intelligent, kind, and also had the rare quality of actually listening to what people said. Women liked him. He had very few close friends and, I sometimes think, no intimate ones. He almost never spoke of his deepest feelings; I think I might be the only person apart from my mother to whom he did. But that did not make him seem a closed or secretive man, merely a private one.

The material comfort he provided for his family was a source of pride to him. He once told me, 'I like the feeling that if I wanted to go down to London and stay at the Ritz for a night or two, you know, I could.' Not that he ever did, but I know what he meant: he liked the wiggle room, the psychic sense of space, that earning a good living brought. This sense of potential freedom came at the cost of mortgaging his life away—but at least in some sense he felt free. He was proud of the good education I was getting, and very proud when I got into Oxford, and then even more proud when I got a first in my moderations, the exams at the end of my first year. He saw this, with reason, as a set of opportunities he had created. When my mother told me about my father's pride in these things, she would always use the same phrase: 'He opened the window and flung his chest out.'

In 1979, having spent thirty years with the same employer, my father had the option of taking early retirement. This might seem like a no-brainer: to have got to the age of fifty-three and now to be free of a job you are bored by, on a comfortable pension, free to do anything you wanted with the rest of your life. What's not to like? It was difficult for my father, though, because it meant accepting that he wasn't going to get any further at the bank and therefore that his career ambition had failed. So taking retirement involved facing and accepting the fact that he was disappointed. He decided to do it anyway, and 1979 was our last year in Hong Kong. Rather than take a summer holiday in England he worked through and left the territory forever in September. I went back to boarding school in England to start my A-level year, and my parents took the long, slow trip home which they had been discussing ever since he decided to stop working: Thailand, Cyprus, and then Sweden to buy a new Saab and drive it home across northern Europe. At school I received a sequence of postcards. And then my parents arrived in Norfolk, some time in early November, and the open-ended years of retirement began.

This was at Alderfen, a house he and my mother bought in 1972. There was no connection of any sort with Norfolk other than the fact that my mother's sister lived in Norwich. In many ways it was an unfortunate choice. Village life proved to be unfriendly even by the standards of English village life—read: very unfriendly indeed. There was next to no culture and no ready-made social life. The site was windy and bleak; the house itself was an unlovely 'chalet bungalow' of recent construction. But my father loved the idea of owning his property, with no street address beyond that one word,

'Alderfen'. It had nineteen acres of land, most of it unusable, indeed unwalkable, marsh; but beautiful nonetheless. It felt like he owned a piece of somewhere. For someone who felt like he didn't belong anywhere and who had lived all his life in property belonging to other people, that was a novel and consoling feeling.

I recently went back to the village and the thought that hit me with great force was: what were they thinking? My father went to a Norfolk village from a highly structured work environment with long hours and a built-in social life in a city where he had lived for most of his life. To go from living in the Tropics, mostly in one of the world's great metropolises, to a sleepy, isolated, insular, cold piece of nowhere—how could it possibly work?

The fact is that my father was entirely unprepared for retirement. As a lively-minded man with many interests, he no doubt thought he would be free of the intellectual underemployment which can blight life after work; he had lived mostly in his head for many years, and probably thought retirement would be more of the same. He began to study electronics on a two-year course at Norwich Technical College, pursuing an interest he had had for years and, characteristically, wanting to find things out from the ground up. (The other mature student doing the course was twenty-four.) When he bought a BBC Microcomputer, one of the first affordable consumer models in the UK, he wanted to know how to program it, and how it worked, software and hardware, from the bare machine-code upwards. I said, 'But what can it do? Who cares how it works?' He shrugged. 'Difference of approach,' he said.

In the summer holiday of 1983, I took him out on the canoe that was my great source of happiness at Alderfen—a neighbour and I would spend hours and hours on the small dykes, the river and the local Broad, the most excitingly wild and natural place I, a city boy, had ever known. On some days we would see a kingfisher that lived near where I kept the canoe: the electric-blue flash of his wings, so startlingly vivid amid all the greens and greys, would, whenever I saw it, be the high spot of my day. I had not known before that a natural phenomenon could be the high spot of a day. At the end of our narrow, overhung mooring, you could turn right and head down to the Broad, or left and explore the narrow, shallow, shifting waterways which were impassable to even a rowing boat. There was never a soul there, except the one day we rescued a man who had got lost (we were in the garage playing darts when we heard him shouting for help—a trick of marsh acoustics, since, when we eventually got to him, he was well over a mile away).

My father didn't often come out in the canoe. Looking back, I think he was worried that the exertion of paddling would overtax his heart. That day, though, it was clear and warm and I managed to get him to come out with me. Instead of heading for the Broad we went down the narrow dyke that ran by the edge of our property—the only way of getting there, since the marsh was too boggy and treacherous to walk. It could have been about 400 yards from our house, no more. The low, overshadowed dyke had been transformed into a broad water avenue, and it only took a moment to see why: about a dozen of the trees on our side of the bank had been cut down. I was surprised and curious, but my father was aghast. We cancelled the day out and went quickly home. A few days later I was back at university. Very soon after that I heard that my parents had put our house on the market and were planning to move.

What had happened was that a few locals had cut the trees down to provide access to the Broad for a mooring down past our property. They knew the trees belonged to us but had done it without asking for the straightforward reason that if they had asked my father might have said no. Quite a few people knew what was happening, but no one thought to tell him. After all he had had the house for only eleven years and had only been living there full-time for three.

The resulting feeling of betrayal was, for my father, very sharp. People he was on nodding and chatting terms with had, he felt, done something behind his back. He had a deep sense of insecurity about the untrustworthiness of the locals; he felt a lack of goodwill. So he sold the house and moved to Norwich.

At the time of my next holiday from university, at Christmas, my mother had gone to Ireland for a week so my father and I had a few days alone together. I had gone home in some triumph, having just won a university prize exam, and Dad was very proud and happy— his own finals result had been, by his own account, the worst day of his life. He was very glad to be in the city. 'It was only when we got here that I realized that I had been so fucking bored,' he said. 'Here you can go out for a drink, you can go for a coffee, you can go to see a film. In the countryside there's just nothing to do.' We went to see Peter Weir's film *The Year of Living Dangerously*, and he said it was uncanny how it caught what Indonesia had been like in the 1950s and 60s. We had dinner together on Wednesday night. On Thursday, my mother came back from Ireland and my girlfriend came to stay for a few days. On Friday my parents went out for a drink after dinner and came back at about nine o'clock. My girlfriend and I were watching Roman Polanski's film *Repulsion* when my father went out of the room. He was gone for about half an hour. My mother went to see what he was doing. She screamed my name. I ran upstairs and saw her standing over my father. 'I think he's died,' she said. My first feeling was a great surge of tenderness for her: I felt so sad for her. Not him, not me—her. I knelt down beside her. She was right. My father was already, not cold, but not live-warm. He had had a massive heart attack.

We buried my father a few days later. The turnout was sparse, since he had so few connections with Norwich. In Hong Kong we could have filled a big church, perhaps even a cathedral. I can remember those days with a terrible clarity. As far as I could tell, I felt nothing, nothing at all. This wasn't denial so much as the fact that I simply couldn't locate my feelings. I just didn't know where they were. And there was so much to do. There were phone calls to make, letters to write, probate to arrange, my mother to look after. I wasn't prepared for anything about death, and one of the things I wasn't prepared for was the sheer workload.

This was the first time I was ever impressed by my mother's religious faith. Her reaction the night my father died was one of pure shock: 'What am I going to do? What will become of me?' she kept saying. But by the next day she was deeply, passionately grieving. She told me that she had always thought it would be her who died first. She was able to feel the loss in a way I simply couldn't, and at the same time I felt it was somehow connected to her ability to see something beyond the loss, a context or meaning, provided by her faith. Somehow, because she could see beyond it, she could also see it—that was how it seemed. As for me, partly because the loss of my father seemed so random, so meaningless other than as pure loss, I couldn't even acknowledge it, much less cope with any of the feelings it brought up. Because I had no way of describing to myself what had happened, it was on some level as if nothing had happened. It was as if I couldn't find my keys; or rather, that I knew I had a pair of keys somewhere, and knew that they would be in some way useful, but couldn't find them. No: it was as if somebody had told me that there was something called a 'key', and that these things called 'keys' were essential, and that I would surely be able to find them if I looked, but I had no idea where they were or what they looked like or even, really, what they were for—just that somewhere, somehow, there were these things I probably needed.

Anthony Powell says somewhere that there's nothing quite like having a father go bankrupt to force a man to think for himself. My father's early death was a version of that. His life was not inherently tragic: he wasn't inherently a sad man. If he had lived to be alive today, aged seventy, he would have had about twenty years of comfortable retirement to balance the years spent doing his boring job. He would, perhaps, have found things he wanted to do—the move into Norwich was a good start. He might have made a new life for himself, or even have just resigned himself to the fact that he was going to potter about enjoying his hobbies. But none of that happened. He didn't have that long balanced life, with years of drudgery evened out by years of suiting himself; he had a truncated life, with years of drudgery followed by an untimely death. That made me determined not to do what he did. Whatever else I did with my working life I wasn't going to spend it doing something I hated.

□

YEAR OF
THE MONKEY
Fan Wu

Two thousand and four, the year of the monkey, my zodiac year. Two weeks before the New Year, Old Aunt Li stopped me on my way home and told me to buy a red rope. 'Tie it around your waist,' she said. 'That'll get rid of bad luck.' She was the self-appointed director of the Community Management Committee in our building and knew everyone's birthday and every family's private business. According to her, in your zodiac year you are either prosperous or miserable. Aunt Li was in her sixties. Unlike other women her age who were busy caring for grandchildren or practising group dance in a park, she would walk around with a thread-bound *I Ching* and replica ancient copper coins in her pocket. It was said she had predicted that Four-eyed Wang's son would get into Beijing University, that rice would cost twenty per cent more by the end of the year and that Doctor Deng on the first floor would have a baby girl.

I didn't believe Aunt Li could foresee the future, but I respected her because she could recite *I Ching* in reverse order. If she had asked me to worship the gods in Temple You Ming every few months, I would have obeyed. But a thirty-six-year-old man with a red rope around his waist? I wasn't ready for that.

Exactly a week after New Year's Eve, when the moon shrank into a crescent, my right eyelid began to twitch. Sometimes it happened when I was brushing my teeth, sometimes when I had squeezed myself on to the bus to work or when I was conversing with a colleague. At first, I didn't care. My eye wasn't red or swollen. I was sure it would go back to normal in a few days. My eyelids had twitched before— when I hadn't had enough sleep or my eyes were tired from my work at the newspaper. Or it might be that I needed new glasses.

One evening, shortly after I went to bed, I felt my right eyelid twitch again—it was as if someone were bouncing a ball up and down in there. After tossing and turning for half an hour, I opened my eyes. In the quiet night, the throbbing seemed audible, the kind of sound you hear from a stethoscope—hollow, yet clear. I pressed my index finger on my eyelid. I stared at the ceiling, counting the throbs silently. A heavy storm had just ended. From time to time a car drove by, its wet tyres skidding on the road like a person weeping. When I reached one hundred, I touched my wife's shoulder.

'Wanyu,' I said. She had her back to me, legs tucked up in a foetal position. This meant she was awake. When she fell asleep, she lay

111

on her back with hands stretched out and her fingers spread apart like an orchid flower. Since the bed was small, one of her hands was often on my stomach, the other hanging over the edge of the bed. She didn't answer and only inched towards the other side of the bed. Her eyes must be open; she'd have fallen from the bed if she moved any further. I touched her shoulder and said her name again.

'Are you going crazy, at this time of night?' she said, still keeping her back to me. She must have thought I wanted to make love. I didn't. The last time we made love was a year ago. Now I was used to masturbation. Wanyu went to work half an hour earlier than I did and I masturbated in that half-hour. Once she caught me. Right before I finished, she came back. She leaned against the door frame, arms crossed, staring at me expressionlessly. Then she shook her head in disgust, walked into the room to fetch the door key she had left on the television, and walked out.

Perhaps that was the day she began looking for a lover.

Now, lying on the bed, I gazed at her back. It was dark in the room, but I could see her bony silhouette under the thin blanket. I imagined her crumpled pyjamas stained with oil and soy sauce—she cooked in her pyjamas, so she wouldn't dirty her day clothes—and her small breasts. I suddenly felt a gentleness in my heart that I hadn't felt in a long time.

'My eyelid keeps twitching,' I said. I touched her shoulder once more. If she turned to me, I thought, I would kiss her. I would kiss her shoulders, her cheeks, the small patches behind her ears, then her lips, just as when we were first married.

She didn't move. 'Right eyelid?' she asked indifferently.

I nodded and withdrew my hand. Of course, she knew as well as I did the old Chinese saying: *If the left eyelid twitches, you have good fortune; if the right eyelid twitches, you go to hell.*

She still didn't turn to look at me, but she seemed to know that I was nodding. 'A person cannot expect to have good luck forever.' She snorted and pulled her blanket up to cover her neck. We had slept under separate blankets for two years, ever since she had caught me with Wei Qing in a park. I didn't mind that: we didn't have to fight for one blanket in winter. Also, our son, Lulu, was only four years old then and liked to sleep with us when it was cold. This week he was staying with Wanyu's parents.

About a year ago I saw Wanyu and a tall man kissing in the same park where Qing and I used to hang out. She stood almost on her tiptoes, her head tilted back and her hair, which she usually wore in a ponytail, was loose and wavy. She was wearing a pink dress I'd never seen before. It fluttered in the wind like a flamingo opening its wings. It had been a long time since I had seen her look so beautiful. I hid behind a tree only a few yards away. They chatted, kissed, cuddled, then left the park with their arms around each other's waists.

That evening I called a newly divorced colleague and went to a bar with him. He flirted with the waitresses and pinched their butts when they served us drinks. He told me he had never been as happy in his life. 'I have nothing to fear,' he said. I didn't leave until he was drunk and sobbing between drinks. It was almost 3 a.m. when I got home. Wanyu had fallen asleep, her arms stretched out wildly, taking up the whole bed, a trace of a smile—or so I thought—in the corners of her mouth.

When she had said, 'A person cannot expect to have good luck forever,' I knew she still remembered those times when I did have good luck. Years ago, in the college entrance examination, my total score was ten points below the admittance threshold. But a reputable college happened to lower its admittance standard that year and I was the last student they accepted. Four years later, at graduation time, the job market was at its worst for teachers of literature. There were only a few city-based openings for my whole class. For a person with only average grades, like me, the best opportunity was teaching in a nearby town. I even thought I would be assigned to the countryside. Then one day the Dean announced that a newspaper was looking for an editor. Everyone was excited about it. The morning the recruiter from the newspaper was due to interview my class I lay on the lawn near a lake, reading 'Dream of the Red Chamber'. Between pages, I thought of my future, and decided that living a life of idleness wasn't unattractive. I would make less money teaching at a county-level school, but the cost of living would be lower outside the city.

A middle-aged man, obviously a visitor, asked me for directions to the building where my department was. I offered to walk him there. We started talking and he told me about the fishing village in Fujian Province where he grew up. My father was born in that village. He and the visitor had gone to the same elementary and high schools.

I had even visited the village a few times as I still had relatives there. I didn't realize it then, but the visitor was the recruiter from the newspaper. When he arrived at my department he asked for me at once without interviewing any of my classmates. Everyone in my class thought I knew powerful people in the government.

On my second date with Wanyu I told her these stories. She laughed. 'God bless good people.' That was what she said. I didn't think she would say that now. I looked at Wanyu's back a little longer. I wanted to get up and smoke but decided not to. It was 2 a.m., the room was dark like a tunnel. Wanyu finally fell asleep with her right arm on my stomach. I listened to her even breathing and counted the throbbing of my eye.

O ur condo building was located in the old town of Nanchang and once belonged to the municipal government. There was a bus station and a park with a fish pond within five minutes' walk. Six years ago, after the municipality had built new apartment buildings for its employees, the condo building was put on the market. The buyers had to be married and at least one of the couple's parents had to be working for the government. 'Let's get married. Let's buy an apartment,' Wanyu said to me one day. We had dated for only five months, but she was twenty-eight and I was thirty. Why wait? Neither of my parents worked for the government, but Wanyu's father was a government-employed mailman, though not a full-time employee. Wanyu and I were allowed to take part in the lottery after her father bribed the person in charge of selling the condos. We waited in line for two days and drew the lottery three times, and finally got a two-bedroom, one-bathroom apartment. My colleagues admired my luck.

But times changed. A year later, the government moved to the more prosperous and convenient New District. As soon as they moved, cleaners started to ignore the park and the water lilies and goldfish in the pond died. The garbage collectors wouldn't pick up until the fifth or sixth call. New District was close to the freeway and every single bus station there had glass ceilings and wooden benches. It also had a musical fountain and two brand-new shopping malls. Wanyu wanted to move to New District but real estate there had tripled in the past few years. Despite our two salaries—mine as a newspaper editor and hers as an accountant in a state-run company—we wouldn't have enough for a down payment even if we saved for ten years. But in my opinion we should have been content: our house was in the centre of the city. Most of my colleagues lived on the outskirts, where the bus services were irregular.

When Lulu was a little over a year old, Wanyua asked me to give all my salary to her every month. 'For Lulu,' she said. It's not in my nature to argue. That was when I began to smoke. The money came out of my quarterly bonus, which everybody in my office got if they took fewer than five sick days.

Wanyu often praised me before her colleagues and friends, saying that I was honest and down to earth. Later, when she was fed up with me she said I was useless, a loser—I had to depend on her father to get our condo; I didn't make enough money to buy a house in New District; I hadn't been promoted after working for the same newspaper for years; I didn't know how to fix a leaking toilet or unclog sinks; Lulu had to go to an average kindergarten as I didn't have the right connections. I didn't defend myself. What could I say? After she found out about my affair with Wei Qing, she said I was sneaky, a fox in rabbit's skin.

Three weeks after my eyelid began to twitch, I went to the emergency unit at the municipal hospital. Before I could finish telling the doctor about my eyelid, I felt it quiver faintly. I wanted to ask the doctor if he believed in the saying 'If the left eyelid twitches, you have good fortune; if the right eyelid twitches, you go to hell.' But doctors aren't fortune-tellers.

He took a tiny yellow flashlight from between a bottle of blue ink and a pile of cotton patches. He switched on the light and examined my right eye. He told me to rotate my eyeball: 'Up...down...left...right...' I rolled it as far as I could, thinking it would help with the diagnosis. The doctor seemed to be annoyed by my effort. 'Enough, that's enough. Now let me see the left eye.' I barely rolled my left eyeball for half a circle before he switched off the flashlight. 'Nothing serious. Exercise your eyeballs every half an hour and you'll be fine in a few days.'

'I've been rolling my eyeballs for half a month.'

'Muscle stress. Just do the same thing for another few days and you'll be okay.'

'Don't I need medicine?'

He glanced at me, smiling for the first time. I knew what was on his mind: he thought I was trying to take advantage of my medical benefits to claim free medicine. He scribbled something on a piece of white paper and gave it to me. I took his prescription: two boxes of traditional medicine used to regulate women's periods and a big bag of herbs to relieve summer heat.

The throbbing of my eyelid annoyed me. I slept poorly and often felt tired at work. One day, Kao, the head of the arts and entertainment section, called me into his office. He asked if I had had a fight with Wanyu, or if Lulu was sick. I said no, everything was fine at home. He took out a thick stack of manuscripts that I had edited and pointed out my mistakes. 'You've been working here for over ten years. You're a senior editor, an old comrade, you know,' he said, patting my shoulder with his fat hand. In the office, among the people under forty years old, I was the only one he called 'an old comrade'. Sometimes I was tempted to ask him if I really looked old. Kao was two years younger than I was and he had been assigned to the newspaper by the government. Before he came, Wanyu thought I had a chance for a promotion. She gave me 300 yuan and asked me to send two bottles of Maotai to the Editor-in-Chief. I spent the money on three packs of Great China cigarettes for myself.

I started to entertain myself by counting the intervals between one twitch and the next. If I was reading, my eyelid would twitch every third page. Even when I deliberately slowed down or speeded up, it followed the same pattern—one twitch every three pages. If I was talking to a colleague, it twitched just before I finished a sentence. If I suddenly stopped in the middle of a sentence, it twitched when the next-to-last word was out of my mouth. When I was riding my bike, it twitched only when I stopped to wait for a green light. In the evenings, it was most active between midnight and 2 a.m., when it twitched every five minutes. The throbbing during these hours was sudden and powerful; I could almost hear it. Between 2 a.m. and 6 a.m., it twitched only once every thirty minutes or so, slowly and carefully, as if there was a small timid animal tiptoeing behind my eye. I lay on the bed until dawn like this, half awake, half asleep.

Perhaps I was a superman with a secret talent? I decided to record the throbbing in a notebook, as a scientist would earthquakes or volcanic eruptions. Duration was measured by the second, and strength on a scale of 1 (the weakest) to 5 (the strongest). At night I put the notebook next to my pillow so I could record my eyelid's activity. I thought that if I were persistent, I might be able to use my research results to predict weather, commodity prices, the stock market, and even the lottery. For the first time I dreamed of becoming rich. I fantasized about quitting my job and travelling abroad—Florence, Athens, then Cairo and Sydney. Of course, before I left, I would buy a house for Wanyu and Lulu in New District.

After a few weeks, I analysed the data in my notebook. I designed dozens of charts and graphs. But apart from discovering that the throbbing increased dramatically the day before thunderstorms, I could find no detectable patterns.

Wanyu went to stay with her parents. Lulu was still there although we had originally agreed that he would visit his grandparents for only a week. On the evening I was going to pick him up, Wanyu dragged a big suitcase from underneath the bed. 'I need to get away for a while,' she said. She tilted her head and stared at me warily, as if I might try to snatch the suitcase from her.

'Let me help you pack,' I said.

'I'm done with packing.'

I looked at her suitcase and didn't know what to say. 'Let me take you to the bus station,' I offered at last.

'I've called a taxi.'

'How long will you be gone?'

'Depends. Perhaps one or two weeks,' she said, going to the bathroom for her bath towel and toothbrush. A few minutes later I heard the taxi honk its horn outside. After she left, I went to our bedroom. The closet was half empty and all of Wanyu's favourite shoes were missing. It was not the first time she had gone to live with her parents. After she found out about me and Wei Qing, she had taken Lulu there with her. The next day, my father-in-law came to my office. He walked to my desk and slapped me on the cheek. Wei Qing quit two days later. I was the only one in the office who knew that she had decided to leave anyway. She didn't quit because of the humiliation or her worry about gossip—she was too modern for that.

I thought about calling her, but I delayed and delayed, and ended up not calling. She didn't call me, either. I had heard she now owned an advertising company in the New District.

Perhaps Wanyu was consulting her parents about filing for divorce. If that's what she wanted, she could have the house and I would move to the dorm my newspaper provided for its single employees. It shouldn't be difficult to find a bed there. But if she wanted a divorce, she'd have asked for one a long time ago. She always assessed things thoroughly, a habit she was either born with or developed as an accountant. I knew her logic. If we divorced, Lulu would have to live with her and who'd want to marry a divorced woman with a six-year-old child? She couldn't be sure that her new husband would treat Lulu well; he would be laughed at by other children for having divorced parents; two incomes were better than one; and, finally, a divorce would allow me to get together with Wei Qing.

Just as I was about to give up my research and burn my notebook, I made another discovery: I could detect lies! That day I went to the office at nine as usual, poured myself a cup of green tea, and sat down to read the pile of manuscripts on my desk. I knew from experience that I could throw most of them into the garbage bin after reading the opening line. The first year I worked at the newspaper I couldn't sleep well but I soon got over the anxiety of rejecting other people's work and now every manuscript thrown in the garbage brought me happiness. Wanyu once said to me that my job satisfied my low self-esteem and my desire for power.

At lunchtime, Kao asked me to see him in his office. After I sat down, he handed me a manila envelope. 'Old Liu, you're an old comrade. You're careful and reliable, and write well. You're the best editor in our department.'

My eyelid suddenly twitched. 'Whose manuscript is it?' I took the envelope and opened it.

'Nothing serious. It's just some stuff Wenying wrote,' he said, his voice an octave lower. Wenying was his second wife. She was fifteen years younger than him and an aspiring writer.

I skimmed the first few poems. Terrible love poems which could have been written by a schoolgirl.

'Quite a few magazines have asked to see her poems.' Kao took out a tin of Oolong and poured some tea for me.

Another heavy throb from my eyelid.

'It'll be our two-year anniversary in another few months. I've promised her, no matter how tight the space is… Old Liu, I trust your insight and talent. You're an old comrade and you know what to do. You just need to edit them. You know how to edit, don't you?' He went back to his black executive chair and crossed his legs. 'By the way, our newspaper isn't doing well this year. Headquarters is considering a layoff. It's confidential and I shouldn't have told you. You needn't edit Wenying's poems if you don't like them. I don't want you to feel any pressure…'

The throbbing was driving me crazy. 'I know what to do,' I said.

'I'm glad to hear that.' He leaned forward. 'You haven't had a raise for three years. This year, I'll put in some good words for you to the Editor-in-Chief. You're an old comrade. You deserve it.'

I stood up, covering my right eye. I could almost hear the throbbing.

'A problem with your eye?'

'Nothing. It's just a little dry.'

That evening I burned the poems. If Kao asked, I would tell him I had been robbed on my way home and the thief had taken the briefcase where I kept the manuscript.

Wanyu came back from her parents. That Sunday I told her that I would do the grocery shopping. Usually she did it—she complained that the meat I bought was too fatty and that the vegetables looked good outside but were all rotten inside.

The farmers' market was right behind our condo building. The road there was always slippery and every few steps you could see small piles of rotten vegetables abandoned by the vendors. Flies buzzed around. I was determined I would buy meat only from an honest trader. I walked from one stand to another, bombarding the traders with questions: 'Did you use needles to inject water into the meat to make it heavier? Why does the meat look so dark? Is it fresh? Is this pork loin? Why is there so much fat? Did you give me the best price? I always buy meat from you. Have you ever given me the right amount?'

My eyelid hurt every time I got an answer. My heartbeat quickened and my brain seemed to be exploding. I became more and more irritated, more and more impatient. By the time I got to the last stand I was almost yelling. The vendor, no more than sixteen years old, looked at me fearfully. He backed away a few steps and into a bloody pig's head. Suddenly it was quiet in the market. Everybody was looking at me and some were whispering. 'Bastard! You're all goddamned bastards!' I said in my heart, then turned to the vendor. 'Cut three jin of lean meat for me!' It felt good to speak like a hooligan. The vendor didn't move. He stared at me until his next-stand neighbour walked over and pushed him. 'Are you deaf? Cut meat for this gentleman! He must be from the Market Management Bureau.' The boyish-looking vendor walked forward slowly and took a piece of lean meat from under the table with trembling hands. He cut at least five jin of meat and, without weighing it, wrapped it with newspaper, and put it into my basket.

I couldn't sleep that night. At 3 a.m. I got up to see Lulu in his room. He was in a deep sleep, mouth half open. Half of his blanket was on the floor. He must have felt cold as his hands were clenched into fists over his chest. I covered him with the blanket, then sat on the edge of the bed to look at him in the street light. When he was a baby, Wanyu and I often argued over who he resembled. That was in the days when we still made love and I didn't smoke. She insisted that his eyes, nose, mouth, eyebrows and chin were hers. The only feature that was mine, she said, was his forehead. She sighed, afraid that Lulu would have my Yu Mu brain, stubborn and inflexible. Now, as I was looking at Lulu, I could see that the only feature from his mother were his eyes, double-lidded, big and bright. His bony nose, thick lips, square chin, and thick brows were all mine. I stroked his forehead. It was the same as mine. Flat and wide. But Lulu was a smart boy and didn't have my Yu Mu brain. Everyone in the neighbourhood loved to play with him.

I went back to bed and looked at Wanyu. She had her back to me and was cocooned in her blanket from her neck to her toes. 'How's Lulu?' she suddenly said in a soft voice.

'He kicked off the blanket again.'

'You can't sleep?'

'You're awake, too.' I put my hand on her waist and tried to turn her to face me.

She didn't follow my hand. After a few seconds' silence, she said, 'We have to work tomorrow. Let's sleep.'

'Wanyu,' I said, without removing my hand. 'Wanyu, do you remember the first year we had Lulu?'

She nodded faintly.

'We were happy, weren't we?'

'I guess so.'

My eyelid didn't twitch. I suddenly couldn't control myself. 'I know I'm not the kind of person who does well wherever he goes. I don't make much money, I don't have connections, I don't like to ask people for favours. I'm lazy, I like dreaming, I'm not handy. I smoke. But...' I couldn't continue. But what? I didn't know.

She tilted her shoulder but still didn't turn round. When I had counted to ten, she said, 'Let's sleep.'

I wanted to ask her if she had decided not to talk to me, not to make love to me for the rest of her life. I wanted to ask her if our lives together would be like this until we died: we would go to work, make money to pay for water, electricity, food, and gas, to pay for Lulu's education from kindergarten to college. We would save for his wedding, his house, and his children. We would work in the same place until we were sixty-five. Then we would retire and go to the park every day to practise Qi Gong or find someone to play chess with. I wanted to ask her what her lover's name was, where he worked, how long they had been together. Why didn't she divorce me? Was he married? Did he have a child? If she cried and apologized, I would say, It's not a big deal: who doesn't have an affair nowadays? Perhaps I would even say something funny: You're so pretty and your husband is so ugly. It'd be odd if other men didn't pursue you.

But I didn't say anything at all. I just stared at her back.

The next afternoon, I left the office without telling anyone. It was the first time that I had sneaked out. Some of my colleagues often found excuses not to come to work or to go home early: Young Li's kid was always sick, Old Wu often had appointments with a plumber or a technician at home, Old Qian couldn't get up on rainy days because of arthritis; I had met Old Qian on the street a few times on rainy weekends and he looked fine to me. Whenever they had to go home early or didn't come in at all, I did the work they hadn't finished. Kao would say to me: 'You're an old comrade. I trust you.'

I rode my bike along Plaza Street to Riverside Boulevard. Twenty minutes later, I arrived at People's Park, where Wanyu caught me with Wei Qing and where I saw her and her lover. Starting last month, the government had banned municipal parks from charging an entrance fee. The park, which once had been so quiet, swarmed with retired people. Men were playing chess. Women disco-danced, or played with their grandchildren. There were people circling the lake, walking backwards—it was said that walking backwards was good for the kidneys and heart.

I suddenly missed Qing—her long fingers and her single-lidded eyes that blinked often. I didn't love her, just as she didn't love me. She stayed only eight months at the newspaper before quitting. Our time together was even shorter, only two months. Not long after she was assigned to my team she began to tell me about herself. She said I looked like an honest person. It was so hard to find an honest person nowadays. She told me everything: She went to bed with a professor at college, her parents divorced when she was in high school, her businessman boyfriend slept with other women when he was on trips. She said she hated this city, where people were trivial, vulgar, and gossipy. She wanted to go to Shanghai and open an interior design company there. She told me the date that she was planning to leave.

I began to tell her a little about my past. I told her I was bullied a lot when I was a kid because I wore thick glasses, and because of this my parents didn't want to have another kid. I told her that I fell in love with a middle-school classmate whose father was my maths teacher. I wrote the girl a love letter every night but burned it as soon as I had finished it. I was never brave enough to show her the letters. A year later, she died of leukaemia. The week before she died, I went to see her with the other classmates. I stood in the last row and looked at her but I didn't dare speak.

After one of these conversations Qing suddenly leaned forward to kiss me. Later she laughed at me and said it took me over ten seconds to react to her kiss. We kissed on a few other occasions but we never had sex. Once she took my hand and put it on her chest. But I only hugged her. I hugged her so tight that it took her a while to push me away. 'Why are you so useless? Why are you such a coward? What are you afraid of? Could you do something daring once in your life? I'm not a virgin and I didn't ask you to divorce your wife. I just want to have fun,' she said.

I found a phone booth and dialled her cell phone, which I still remembered. Nobody answered the first time. The second time a man picked up the phone on the sixth ring.

'Is Wei Qing there?' I said after a pause.

'Who are you? Why are you asking for her?' His voice was cold.

'I'm an old colleague of hers from the newspaper she used to work for. I only wanted to say hello.'

Silence, then a few seconds later he said, 'She's busy right now.'

My eyelid twitched before he finished his sentence.

'I just wanted to say hello.'

He hung up. Before the phone went dead, I heard giggling in the background.

I continued on my bike. After passing a few graffitied viaducts, I arrived at the building where I lived when I was a bachelor. It was empty and the red-brick walls had grown dark-green mosses. In another month, this building, along with a few others nearby, would be torn down and become part of an amusement park. The half-finished amusement park was already in operation with a roller coaster, a Ferris wheel and carousels. I brought Lulu here once and rode a roller coaster for the first time. I was sick for the next few days.

I locked my bike and bought an entrance ticket. The radio was broadcasting an advertisement for the attractions; the broadcasters' voices were enticing and urgent. The background music was some kind of heavy metal. It was eight minutes past two, but the park was crowded. There were people from out of town speaking dialects I couldn't comprehend and there were students playing truant.

I stood in front of the roller coaster, whose winding tracks looked like intestines in a demon's stomach. I sat down on a bench, smoking the last pack of the expensive cigarettes I bought with the 300 yuan Wanyu had given me. I queued behind the students for a ticket for the roller coaster. Before I went on, I asked the ticket-seller, 'Is this ride safe?' He replied without raising his head from the tabloid entertainment magazine he was reading, 'It's safer than you staying in your house. It was imported from the United States and installed by Japanese. You cannot find a safer place than this.' I waited until my eyelid stopped throbbing, then found a seat in the first row.

The car started to move and soon I was soaked with cold sweat. The friction between the wheels and the track was tearing my head apart. I kept my eyes open, one hand holding my glasses, the other grabbing the door frame. I looked at the sky and the ground spinning before me. My mouth was filled with sour saliva and I felt my heart could stop beating any minute—I wished it would. Then the last dive began, from the highest to the lowest point. The students beside me all raised their hands and screamed with laughter. I raised my hands, too, and I laughed with them and louder than them to conceal my fear, to fit in. As soon as I started to laugh, I felt better. So I laughed even more hysterically. In my delirium, my glasses flew off my face. I saw nothing but a foggy blankness before me and around me. But I didn't care. I kept laughing. □

LONG LANE
with *Turnings*

Last Words of a Motoring Legend

L.J.K. SETRIGHT

Introduction by Michael Bywater
Afterword by James May

'The doyen of British motoring writers …
He found it impossible to be boring'
Alan Judd, *Spectator*

GRANTA BOOKS

Hardback• £12.99 • www.granta.com

ALBERT SMITH
Graham Smith

Graham Smith

My dad, George Albert Newton Smith, was born into a family whose culture, work and class were rooted deep in the heavy industry of ironmaking. In hope of a better life, his great grandfather left the ironstone mines at Rosedale during the middle of the nineteenth century to look for work in the fast growing industrial town of Middlesbrough. He was the first of four generations to work for the powerful ironmasters who, with their vision of an iron and steel metropolis, built so many blast furnaces along the River Tees that it was said one man could not count them all in one day. There was a job for any man who had the strength to work and the will to give loyalty for life to the company. As a young boy older than his years my dad knew that when his days at school ended, by tradition he would follow his own dad into the Cargo Fleet Iron Company. Working together under the structure of three formidable blast furnaces, they repaired the large steam cranes used for moving ironstone and slag. His older brother Bill worked as a front man at the foot of one of those blast furnaces, but some years later was crushed to death when the ageing furnace, under too much pressure, exploded.

Cargo Fleet was about one mile from where the family lived in South Bank. Opposite their house in North Street, just over a high slagstone wall, was an industrial landscape that followed the river as far as they could see. On days with no wind, polluted air glittered with metallic dust from furnaces producing iron day and night, coke ovens and slag tips leaked their stench of sulphurous gas, and the continual clatter of wagons echoed off a vast complex of railway lines, veins feeding every part of the industry. Somewhere on that ironworks land my dad worked an allotment and kept hens. With money made from selling eggs he bought a double format box camera, taught himself how to develop film and make contact prints from negatives. A year later the war started. Taking photographs in public places was prohibited, film was almost impossible to get and he exposed only a few rolls in that first year of owning a camera.

Three months after the war ended he met Hilda Cheesbrough, my mother. She was on her twenty first birthday night out in the Albion pub down Dock Street in Middlesbrough. My dad was there as captain of the visiting darts team from the Princess Alice, South Bank. She was a good looking woman. He bought her that drink.

Albert, back of North Street, South Bank. Just finished work, 1939

Graham Smith

The pleasures of youth, love, children, and a secure job in the ironworks: it was a good time for both of them. They were starting a life together and despite recurring poverty, my dad's photographs confirm how much they were celebrating that life, the love they had for each other and their children. There is a photograph of my mother on the sands at Redcar taken at the beginning of those years, wearing a blouse and skirt she lovingly embroidered with floral hearts.

Those years passed. Three growing children, debt, my mother's late night job as a barmaid and the routine grind for my dad working all the overtime hours he could get, turned their life into one they had no time or desire to continue celebrating. What few photographs my dad was motivated to take of the family became weaker as domestic friction infected their lives with bitterness. Drink was no medicine for the pain they suffered. My mam and dad struggled to keep their heads above water, and life together gradually became one of survival with little comfort from love. Good times still surprised us all, but not often and not for long.

At about the age of eight I made a mousetrap from my dad's box camera. In my child's mind the mousetrap had a use. His neglected camera, which was almost beyond reach on the top shelf of our pantry, was never replaced. The photographs stopped.

Four or five bad years later, the County Court issued an Order of Legal Separation against my dad for mental cruelty towards his children. An unfair ruling by a judge blind to the provocation from a woman my dad never stopped loving. The judge also ordered that he had just forty eight hours to pack up and get out of his home for good.

Apart from his tools and a suit of clothes my dad had no personal belongings that I can remember, no books, not even the box camera he brought into the marriage, only his negatives and a small family photo album, half full. During those forty eight hours and for a long time after, he was in a state of shock, his sense of purpose lost in despair. I can still remember the day he came home from work looking tired as if he had just finished a double shift under the furnaces. No words were spoken, it was hard to look at him or be in the same room, he was offered nothing to eat and what bits of food we had in the pantry were hidden away. We even burned off what was left of a shilling's worth of gas in the coin meter just in case he tried to make a cup of tea. He washed in silence, packed a small case, filled a brown paper carrier bag with dirty work clothes, and without looking up to say goodbye, left his home, wife and three children. On that sunny evening, I followed a man walking slowly through our alley on to Keith Road and, hiding in the shadows of our neighbour's privet hedge, watched him disappear down the road towards the bus stop. He never again set foot inside the house that was his home. Although he found lodgings only a few miles away in South Bank, I didn't see my dad again for what turned out to be eight disturbing years. Remnants he left behind were gathered up by my mother and triumphantly thrown away. Our bin was kept outside the back door and that week it was full. Next to the bin among a heap of worn out work clothes, old boots and some unfinished wooden toys I found the cardboard shoebox full of my dad's carefully cut single negatives. Although each one was scratched and many bent or sticky with jam from the years we had played with those mysterious pictures, they were a part of my life. But whatever hope that box full of better days gave me it was empty for those two very special people on that awful and final day we were a family. One of the rare times I knew without doubt that I had done something right was on bin men day when, before leaving for school, I salvaged the box of negatives and hid them in a dark corner on the top shelf of our pantry, well away from the nerves of my mother.

Most of the negatives were moments from the best years of both my mam and dad's long life, going back to the night down Dock Street when he bought her that drink, up to a time when his last photograph of family life found a place in the shoe box.

Albert's dad George, North Street, 1939

Albert's mother Ruth with her first grandson George. His dad, Albert's brother Bill, was killed not long after this photograph was taken. Back yard, North Street, 1939

Nelson Street, between North Street and Middlesbrough Road. Clay Lane furnaces, South Bank, 1969. Photograph Graham Smith.

Ruth and grandson George, just orphaned after his mother died of cancer, North Street, 1944/5.

Harry Henderson, Albert's cousin and Graham's godfather, back of North Street, 1944/5

Next door neighbour's child, back of North Street, 1944/5

Ruth outside their house, North Street, 1944/5

Albert's wife Hilda, Redcar sands, 1947

Hilda with Sheila and Graham on a rocking horse Albert made. Back garden of
council house, Keith Road, Middlesbrough, 1949

Albert with Sheila, his niece Marleen and Graham, living room, Keith Road, 1950

Albert with Graham, Redcar sands, 1948

Hilda with Sheila and Graham, Redcar sands, 1948

Hilda with youngest son Andrew, Redcar sands, 1951

Sheila and Graham, Albert Park, Middlesbrough, 1950

Sheila, Graham and Andrew with Albert's sister Mary, Ann Street, South Bank, 1950

Sheila and Graham, living room, Keith Road, Middlesbrough, 1953

Graham, Andrew and Sheila. Ship grounded on Redcar rocks, 1953

Clay Lane furnaces, South Bank, 1978. Photograph Graham Smith

The Black Path
and the derelict
Cargo Fleet Iron
Works, looking
towards Clay Lane
furnaces, South
Bank 1982.
Photograph
Graham Smith

Canteen, Clay Lane
furnaces, South
Bank, 1982.
Photograph
Graham Smith

Bennett's Corner,
Middlesbrough Road,
South Bank, 1982.
Photograph
Graham Smith

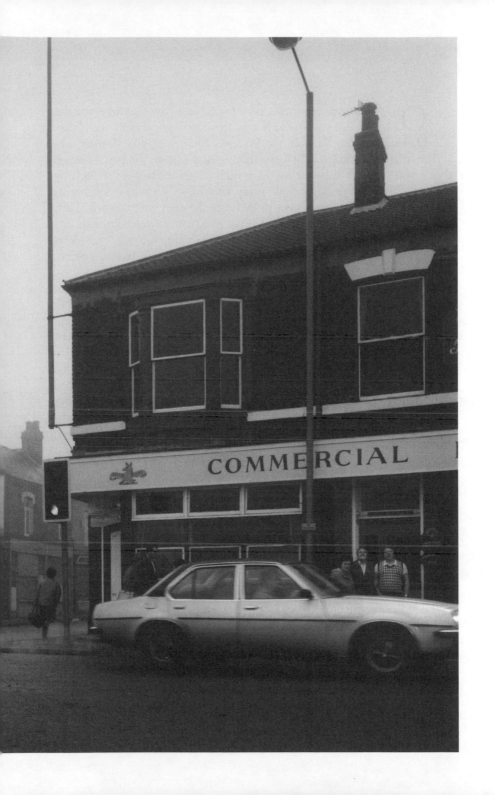

Graham Smith

Only forty four years old and a proud man, my dad accepted that his marriage was over. He was also a strong man and once talked of street fighting outside the Princess Alice with any drinker who matched his challenge of a ten shilling note put on the bar. Although it was a tough way for a young man to get extra beer money, the eviction from his home and family later in life hit him much harder. The only way he knew how to live with the grief was to work. There were exceptions but eventually he worked every twelve hour shift he could get, seven days a week year after year. He no longer considered such endless hours as overtime. Hard work was in his blood, it earned him respect and gave some purpose to the rest of his life.

For more than twenty years, my dad went back to an empty house at the end of a long day's work. With the urgency of closing time on his mind, he fed the cats, cooked himself something from a tin, washed, and dressed in a smart suit that lifted his mood. He depended on pubs for his social life and enjoyed a good drink. The warning bell followed by those sharp words from a barmaid 'last orders please' were an unsettling reminder that good times end. Always the last to leave the pub, three more pints and ten minutes drinking-up time closed down most of his days. His open face, warm smile and sense of humour were well known and well liked. Albert's company was looked for in whichever local pub kept the best pint of beer. He embraced strangers, particularly women, yet my mother was to be the only woman in his life. Although his experience of love became confused with feelings of anger and hate, I found two small racing diaries after his death, each with a photograph of her inside the plastic cover. These two photographs, treasured but painful reminders of the love they once shared, were pulled from the family album knowing at the time that life would never be as it was at the end of his next day's shift. Our dad did not come home from work again. Many years later I got to know a little of who my dad was, and I think the love and belonging he left behind in that shoebox full of negatives were all he ever wanted from life.

Living on his own for so long my dad eventually felt the need to keep a diary. Over ten years he filled two exercise books and started a third, recording important information and events in his life. His last entry noted the weather getting colder, that he'd finished making a garden bench and cleared tomato plants from the greenhouse, that

Albert with Graham's son Gary, the Princess Alice, South Bank, 1985. Photograph Graham Smith

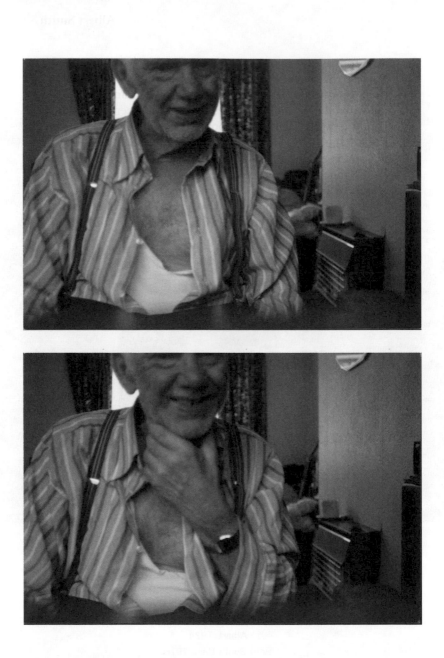

there was too much cigarette smoke in local pubs, and, 'Health getting worse this week, difficulty in breathing after any exertion'. That same week he also left two self portraits in his camera, pictures of a man with a brave smile and eyes lost for a moment somewhere far beyond the walls of his living room. To leave loved ones such a gift was how much he valued photography. He used it well. It was a sad and unexpected phone call. My dad's heart suffered from the stress of too much overtime and stopped working. He died getting into his old car outside the bookies on Middlesbrough Road, only two streets away from where he was born. No betting slip was found, so either he was collecting winnings or, after studying the form, didn't fancy his chances that day. □

Albert, 1924.
Born South Bank 1916.
Died South Bank 1989.

JUMPING
MONKEY HILL
Chimamanda Ngozi Adichie

The cabins all had thatch roofs. Names like BABOON LODGE and PORCUPINE PLACE were hand-painted beside the wooden doors that led out to cobblestone paths and the windows were left open so that guests woke up to the rustling of the jacaranda leaves and the steady calming crash of the sea's waves. The wicker trays held a selection of fine teas. At mid-morning, discreet black maids made the beds, cleaned the elegant standing bathtubs, vacuumed the carpet and left wild flowers in hand-crafted vases. Ujunwa found it odd that the African Writers' Workshop was held here, at Jumping Monkey Hill. The name itself was incongruous, and the resort had the complacence of the well fed about it, the kind of place where she imagined affluent foreign tourists would dart around taking pictures of lizards and then return home still unaware that there were more black people than red-capped lizards in South Africa. Later, she would learn that Edward Campbell chose the resort; he had spent weekends there when he was a lecturer at the University of Cape Town years ago.

But she didn't know this the afternoon Edward picked her up at the airport, an old man in a summer hat who smiled to show two front teeth the colour of mildew. He kissed her on both cheeks. He asked if she had had any trouble with her pre-paid ticket in Lagos, if she minded waiting for the Ugandan whose flight would come soon, if she was hungry. He told her that his wife, Hillary, had already picked up most of the other workshop participants and that their friends, Jason and Sarah, who had come with them from London as paid staff, were arranging a welcome lunch back at the resort. They sat down. He balanced the sign with the Ugandan's name on his shoulder and told her how humid Cape Town was at this time of the year, how pleased he was about the workshop arrangements. He lengthened his words. His accent was what the British called posh, the kind some rich Nigerians tried to mimic and ended up sounding unintentionally funny.

Ujunwa wondered if he had selected her for the workshop. Probably not; it was the British Council that had made the call for entries and then selected the best. Edward had moved a little and sat closer to her on the airport bench. He was asking what she did back home in Nigeria. Ujunwa faked a wide yawn and hoped he would stop talking. He repeated his question and asked whether she had taken leave from her job to attend the workshop. He was watching her intently. He could be anything from sixty-five to ninety.

She could not tell his age from his face; it was pleasant but unformed, as though God, having created him, had slapped him flat against a wall and smeared his features all over his face. She smiled vaguely and said that she had just lost her job before she left—a job in banking—and so there had been no need to take leave. She yawned again. He seemed keen to know more and she did not want to say more and so when she looked up and saw the Ugandan walking towards them, she was very relieved.

The Ugandan looked sleepy. He was square-faced and dark-skinned with uncombed hair that had tightened into kinky balls. He bowed as he shook Edward's hand with both of his and then turned and mumbled a hello to Ujunwa. He sat in the front seat of the Renault. The drive to the resort was long, on roads haphazardly chiselled into steep hills, and Ujunwa worried that Edward was too old to drive so fast. She held her breath until they arrived at the cluster of thatch roofs and manicured paths. A smiling blonde woman showed her to her cabin, Zebra Lair. She sat on the bed and smelled the cool lavender scent from the linen and then got up to unpack, looking out of the window from time to time to search the canopy of trees for lurking monkeys. There were none, unfortunately, Edward told the participants during lunch under pink umbrellas on the terrace, their tables pushed close to the railings so that they could look down at the turquoise sea. He pointed at each person and did the introductions. The white South African woman was from Durban, while the black man came from Johannesburg. The Tanzanian man came from Dar es Salaam, the Ugandan man from Kampala, the Zimbabwean woman from Harare, the Kenyan man from Nairobi, and the Senegalese woman, the youngest at twenty-three, had flown in from Paris, where she was at university.

Edward introduced Ujunwa last—'Ujunwa Ogundu is our Nigerian participant and she lives in Lagos.' Ujunwa looked around the table and wondered with whom she would get along. The Senegalese woman looked most promising, with the irreverent sparkle in her eyes and the Francophone accent and the streaks of silver in her fat dreadlocks. The Zimbabwean woman had longer, thinner dreadlocks and the cowries in them clinked as she moved her head from side to side. She seemed hyper, over-active, and Ujunwa thought she might like her, but only the way she liked alcohol—in small amounts. The Kenyan and Tanzanian men looked ordinary, almost indistinguishable, tall with wide foreheads, wearing tattered beards and short-sleeved shirts. She thought she would like them in the uninvested way that one likes non-threatening people. She wasn't sure about the South Africans—the white woman had a too-earnest face, humourless and free of make-up, and the black man looked patiently pious, like a Jehovah's Witness who went from door to door and smiled when each was shut in his face. As for the Ugandan, she had disliked him from the airport, and even more now with his toady answers to Edward's questions, the way he leaned forward to speak only to Edward and ignored the other participants. They, in turn, said little to him. He was the winner of the last Lipton African Writers' Prize with a prize of fifteen thousand pounds. They didn't include him in the polite talk about their flights.

After they ate the creamy chicken prettied with herbs, after they drank the sparkling water in glossy bottles, Edward stood up to give the welcome address. He squinted as he spoke and the thin hair scattered over his scalp fluttered in the breeze that smelled of the sea. He started by telling them what they already knew—that the workshop would be for two weeks, that it was his idea but of course funded graciously by the Chamberlain Arts Foundation, just as the Lipton African Writers' Prize had been his idea and funded also by the good people at the Chamberlain Foundation, that they were all expected to produce one story for possible publication in the *Oratory*, that laptops would be provided in the cabins, that they would write during the first week and review each participant's work during the second week, and that the Ugandan would be workshop leader. Then he talked about himself, how African literature had been his cause for forty years, a life-long passion that started at Oxford. He glanced often at the Ugandan. The Ugandan nodded eagerly at each glance. Finally, he introduced his wife, Hillary, although they had all met her. He told them she was an animal rights activist, an old Africa hand who had spent her teenage years in Botswana. He looked proud when she stood up, as if her tall and lean gracefulness made up for what he lacked in appearance. Her hair was a muted red, cut so that wisps framed her face. She patted it as she said, 'Edward, really, an introduction.' Ujunwa imagined, though, that Hillary had wanted that introduction, that perhaps she had even reminded Edward of it, saying, 'Now, dear, remember to introduce me properly at lunch.' Her tone would be delicate. The same tone she used the next day at breakfast when she sat next to Ujunwa and said that surely, with that exquisite bone structure, Ujunwa had to come from royal stock in Nigeria. The first thing that came to Ujunwa's mind was to ask if Hillary ever needed royal blood to explain the good looks of friends back in London. She did not ask that, though, and instead said—because she could not resist—that she was indeed a princess and came from an ancient lineage and that one of her forebears had captured a Portuguese trader in the seventeenth century and kept him, pampered and oiled, in a royal cage. She stopped to sip her cranberry juice and smile into her glass. Hillary said, brightly, that she could always spot royal blood and she hoped Ujunwa would support her anti-poaching campaign and it was just horrible, horrible, how many endangered apes people were killing and they didn't even eat them, never mind all that talk about bush meat, they just used the private parts for charms. After breakfast, Ujunwa called her mother and told her about the resort and about Hillary and was pleased when her mother chuckled. She hung up and sat in front of her laptop and thought about how long it had been since her mother really laughed. She sat there for a long time, moving the mouse from side to side, trying to decide whether to name her character something common like Chioma or something exotic like Ibari.

Chioma lives with her mother in Lagos. She has a degree in Economics from Nsukka, has recently finished her National Youth Service and every Thursday she buys the Guardian and scours the employment section and sends out her CV in brown manila envelopes. She hears nothing for weeks. Finally, she gets a phone call inviting her to an interview. After the first few questions, the man says he will hire her and then walks across and stands behind her and reaches over her shoulders to squeeze her breasts. She hisses, 'Stupid man! You cannot respect yourself!' and leaves. Weeks of silence follow. She helps out at her mother's boutique. She sends out more envelopes. At the next interview, the woman tells her she wants somebody foreign-educated, speaking in the fakest, silliest accent Chioma has ever heard and Chioma almost laughs as she leaves. More weeks of silence. Chioma has not seen

her father in months but she decides to go to his new office in
Ikoyi to ask if he can help her find a job. Their meeting is tense.
'Why have you not come since, eh?' he asks, pretending to be
angry, because she knows it is easier for him to be angry, it is easier
to be angry with people after you have hurt them. He makes some
calls. He gives her a thin roll of 200-naira notes. He does not ask
about her mother. She notices that the Yellow Woman's photo is on
his desk. Her mother had described her well—'She is very fair, she
looks mixed, and the thing is that she is not even pretty, she has a
face like an over-ripe yellow pawpaw.'

The main dining room of Jumping Monkey Hill had chandeliers
that hung low over the long white-covered table. Edward sat at
one end, Hillary at the other, and the participants in between. The
hard wood floors thumped noisily as waiters walked around and
handed out menus. Ostrich medallions. Smoked salmon. Chicken in
orange sauce. Edward urged everyone to eat the ostrich. It was
simply *mah-ve-lous*. Ujunwa did not like the idea of eating an ostrich,
did not even know that people ate ostriches, and when she said so,
Edward laughed good-naturedly and said that of course ostrich was
an African staple. Everyone else ordered the ostrich, and when
Ujunwa's chicken came, too tart, she wondered if perhaps she should
have had the ostrich. It looked like beef anyway. She drank more
alcohol than she had ever drunk in her life, two glasses of wine, and
she felt mellowed and chatted with the Senegalese about the best
ways to care for natural black hair. She heard snatches as Edward
talked about wine: Chardonnay was horribly boring.

Afterwards, the participants gathered in the gazebo, except for the
Ugandan, who sat away with Edward and Hillary. They slapped at
flying insects and drank wine and laughed and teased one another.
You Kenyans are too submissive! You Nigerians are too aggressive!
You Tanzanians have no fashion sense! You Senegalese are too
brainwashed by the French! They talked about the war in Sudan,
about the decline of the African Writers Series, about books and
writers. They agreed that Dambudzo Marechera was astonishing, that
Alan Paton was patronizing, that Isak Dinesen was unforgivable. The
Kenyan put on a generic European accent and, between drags at his
cigarette, recited what Isak Dinesen had said about all Kikuyu

children becoming mentally retarded at the age of nine. They laughed. The Zimbabwean said Achebe was boring and did nothing with style and the Kenyan said that was a sacrilege and snatched at the Zimbabwean's wine glass, until she recanted, laughing, saying of course Achebe was sublime. The Senegalese said she nearly vomited when a professor at the Sorbonne told her that Conrad was really on 'her side', as if she could not decide for herself who was on her side. Ujunwa began to jump up and down, babbling nonsense to mimic Conrad's Africans, feeling the sweet lightness of wine in her head. The Zimbabwean laughed and staggered and fell into the water fountain and climbed out spluttering, her dreadlocks wet, saying she had felt some fish wiggling around in there. The Kenyan said he would use that for his story—fish in the fancy resort fountain—since he really had no idea what he was going to write about. The Senegalese said her story was really *her* story, about how she mourned her girlfriend and how her grieving had emboldened her to come out to her parents although they now treated her being a lesbian as a mild joke and continued to speak of the families of suitable young men. The black South African looked alarmed when he heard 'lesbian'. He got up and walked away. The Kenyan said the black South African reminded him of his father, who attended a Holy Spirit Revival church and didn't speak to anybody on the street. The Zimbabwean, Tanzanian, white South African, Senegalese all spoke about their fathers. They looked at Ujunwa and she realized that she was the only one who had said nothing and, for a moment, the wine no longer fogged her mind. She shrugged and mumbled that there was really little to say about her father. He was a normal person. 'Is he in your life?' the Senegalese asked, with the soft tone that meant she assumed he was not.

Ujunwa's resentment surprised her. 'He is in my life,' she said with a quiet force. 'He was the one who bought me books when I was a child and the one who read my early poems and stories.' She paused and everyone was looking at her and she added, 'He did something that surprised me. It hurt me, too, but mostly it surprised me.' The Senegalese looked as if she wanted to ask more, but changed her mind and said she wanted more wine. 'Are you writing about your father?' the Kenyan asked and Ujunwa said an emphatic NO, because she had never believed in fiction as therapy. The Tanzanian told her that all fiction was therapy, some sort of therapy, no matter what anybody said. That evening, Ujunwa tried to write but her eyeballs were swimming and her head was aching and so she went to bed. After breakfast, she sat before the laptop and cradled a cup of tea.

Chioma gets a call from Merchant Trust Bank, one of the places her father contacted. He knows the chairman of the board. She is hopeful; all the bank people she knows drive nice new Jettas and have nice flats in Lekki. The deputy manager interviews her. He is dark and good-looking and his glasses have a designer label and, as he speaks to her, she desperately wishes he would notice her. He doesn't. He tells her that they would like to hire her to do 'PR', which will mean going out and bringing in new accounts. She will be working with Yinka. If she can bring in ten million naira during her trial period, she will be guaranteed a permanent position. She nods as he speaks. She is used to men's attention and is sulky that he does not look at her as a man looks at a woman and she does not quite understand what he means by going out to get new accounts until she starts the job two weeks later. A uniformed driver takes her and Yinka in an air-conditioned official jeep—she runs her hand over the smooth leather seat, breathes in the crisp air, is reluctant to climb out—to the home of an Alhaji in Victoria Island. The Alhaji is avuncular and expansive with his smile, his hand gestures, his laughter. Yinka has already come to see him a few times before and he hugs her and says something that makes her laugh. He looks at Chioma. 'This one is too fine,' he says. A steward serves frosted glasses of chapman. The Alhaji speaks to Yinka but glances often at Chioma. Then he asks Yinka to come closer and explain the high-interest savings accounts to him, and then he asks her to sit on his lap and doesn't she think he's strong enough to carry her? Yinka says of course he is and sits on his lap, smiling a steady smile. Yinka is small and fair; she reminds Chioma of the Yellow Woman.

What Chioma knows of the Yellow Woman is what her mother told her. One slow afternoon, the Yellow Woman had walked into her mother's boutique on Adeniran Ogunsanya Street. Her mother knew who the Yellow Woman was, knew the relationship with her husband had been on for a year, knew that he had paid for the Yellow Woman's Honda Accord and flat in Ilupeju. But what drove her mother crazy was the insult of this: the Yellow Woman coming to her boutique, looking at shoes and planning to pay for them with money that belonged to her husband. So her mother yanked at the Yellow Woman's weave-on that hung to her back and screamed, 'Husband snatcher!' and the salesgirls joined in, slapping and beating the Yellow Woman until she ran out to her car. When Chioma's father heard of it, he shouted at her mother and said she had acted like one of those wild women from the street, had disgraced him, herself and an innocent woman for nothing. Then he left the house. Chioma came back from National Youth Service and noticed her father's wardrobe was empty. Aunty Chika, Aunty Rose, Aunty Uche had all come and said to her mother, 'We are prepared to go with you and beg him to come back home or we will go and beg on your behalf.' Chioma's mother said, 'Never, not in this world. I am not going to beg him. It is enough.' Aunty Funmi came and said the Yellow Woman had tied him up with native medicine and she knew a good *babalawo* who could untie him. Chioma's mother said, 'No, I am not going.' Her boutique was failing because Chioma's father had always helped her import shoes from Dubai and Italy. So she lowered prices, advertised in *Joy* and *City People*, and started stocking good-quality shoes made in Aba. Chioma is wearing a pair of those shoes the morning she sits in the Alhaji's sitting room and watches Yinka perch on the expansive lap, talking about the benefits of a savings account with Merchant Trust Bank.

At first, Ujunwa tried not to notice that Edward often stared at her breasts. The workshop days had taken on a routine of breakfast at eight and lunch at one and dinner at six in the grand dining room. On the sixth day, Edward handed out copies of the first story to be discussed, written by the Zimbabwean. The participants were all seated on the terrace and after he handed out the papers, Ujunwa noticed that all the seats under the umbrellas were occupied. It was hot and sunny.

'I don't mind sitting in the sun,' she said. 'Would you like me to stand up for you, Edward?'

'I'd rather like you to lie down for me,' he said. The moment was humid, thick, a bird cawed from far away. Edward was grinning. The others down the table had not heard him. Then the Ugandan laughed. And Ujunwa laughed because it was funny and witty, she told herself, when you really thought about it. After lunch, she took a walk with the Zimbabwean and as they stopped to pick shells by the sea, Ujunwa wanted to tell her what Edward said. But the Zimbabwean seemed distracted, less chatty than usual; she was probably anxious about her story. Ujunwa read it that evening. She thought the writing had too many flourishes, but she liked the story and wrote appreciations and careful suggestions in the margins. It was familiar and funny, about a Harare secondary school teacher whose Pentecostal minister tells him that he and his wife will not have a child until they get a confession from the witches who have tied up his wife's womb. They become convinced that the witches are their next-door neighbours and every morning they pray loudly, throwing verbal Holy-Ghost bombs across the fence.

There was a short silence around the dining table after the Zimbabwean read an excerpt the next day. The Ugandan spoke finally and said there was much energy in the prose. The white South African nodded enthusiastically. The Kenyan disagreed. Some of the sentences tried so hard to be literary that they didn't make sense, he said, and read one such sentence. The Tanzanian man said a story had to be looked at as a whole and not parts. Yes, the Kenyan agreed, but each part had to make sense in order to form a whole that made sense. Then Edward spoke. The writing was certainly ambitious but the story itself begged the question 'So what?' There was something terribly passé about it when one considered all the other things happening in Zimbabwe under the horrible Mugabe. Ujunwa stared at Edward. What did he mean by passé? How could a story so familiar be passé? But she did not ask what Edward meant and the Kenyan did not ask and the Ugandan did not ask and all the Zimbabwean did was shove her dreadlocks away from her face, cowries clinking. Everyone else remained silent. Soon, they all began to yawn and say goodnight and walk to their cabins.

The next day, they did not talk about the previous evening. Edward sat at the middle of the table. They talked about how fluffy the scrambled eggs were and how eerie the jacaranda leaves that rustled against their windows at night were. After dinner, the Senegalese read from her story. It was a windy night and they shut the windows to keep out the sound of the whirling trees. The smoke from Edward's pipe hung over the room. The Senegalese read two pages of a funeral scene, stopping often to sip some water, her accent thickening as she became more emotional, each *t* sounding like a *z*. Afterwards, everyone turned to Edward, even the Ugandan, who seemed to have forgotten that he was workshop leader. Edward chewed at his pipe thoughtfully before he said that homosexual stories of this sort weren't reflective of Africa, really.

'Which Africa?' Ujunwa blurted out.

The black South African shifted on his seat. Edward chewed further at his pipe. Then he looked at Ujunwa in the way one would look at a child who refused to keep still in church and said that he wasn't speaking as an Oxford-trained Africanist, but as one who was keen on the real Africa and not the imposing of Western ideas on African venues. The Zimbabwean and Tanzanian and white South African began to shake their heads as Edward was speaking.

'How African is it for a person to tell her family that she is homosexual?' Edward asked.

The Senegalese burst out in incomprehensible French and then, a minute of fluid speech later, said, 'I am Senegalese! I am Senegalese!' Edward responded in equally swift French and then said in English, with a soft smile, 'I think she had too much of that excellent Bordeaux,' and the Ugandan laughed too loudly.

Ujunwa was first to leave. She was close to her cabin when she heard somebody call her and she stopped. It was the Kenyan and the Zimbabwean and the white South African. 'Let's go to the bar,' they said. She wondered where the Senegalese was. She drank a glass of wine and listened to them talk about how the other guests at Jumping Monkey Hill—all of whom were white—looked at the participants suspiciously. The Kenyan said a youngish couple had stopped and stepped back a little as he approached them on the path the day before. The white South African said they were suspicious of her, too, perhaps because she wore only kente-print caftans. Sitting there, staring into the black night, listening to drink-softened voices around her, Ujunwa felt a self-loathing burst open in the bottom of her stomach. She should not have laughed when Edward said, 'I'd rather like you to lie down for me.' It had not been funny. It had not been funny at all. She had hated it, hated the grin on his face and the glimpse of greenish teeth and the way he always looked at her chest rather than at her face and yet she had made herself laugh like a deranged hyena. She placed down her half-finished glass of wine and said, 'Edward is always looking at my breasts.' The Kenyan and white South African and Zimbabwean stared at her. Ujunwa repeated herself. Edward is always looking at my breasts. The Kenyan said it was clear from the first day that the man would be climbing on top of that flat stick of a wife and wishing it were Ujunwa; the Zimbabwean said Edward's eyes were always leery on Ujunwa; the white South African said he would never look at a white woman like that because what he felt for Ujunwa was a fancy without respect.

'You all noticed?' Ujunwa asked them. 'You all noticed?' She felt strangely betrayed. She got up and went to her cabin. She called her mother but the metallic voice kept saying, 'The number you are calling is not available at the moment, please try later,' and so she hung up. She could not write. She lay in bed and stayed awake for so long that when she finally fell asleep it was dawn.

It was the Tanzanian's turn the following evening. His story was about the killings in Congo, from a militiaman's point of view, a man full of prurient violence. Edward said it would be the lead story in the *Oratory*, that it was urgent and relevant, that it brought news. Ujunwa thought it read like a piece from *The Economist* with cartoon characters painted in. But she didn't say that. She went back to her cabin and, although she had a stomach ache, she turned on her laptop.

As Chioma sits and stares at Yinka's smiling face, she feels as if she is acting a play. She wrote plays in secondary school. Her class staged one during the school's anniversary celebration and, at the end, there was a standing ovation and the principal said, 'Chioma is our future star!' Her father was there, sitting next to her mother, clapping and smiling. But when she said she wanted to study literature in university, he told her it was not viable. His word, viable. He said she had to study something else and could always write by the side. The Alhaji is lightly rubbing Yinka's arm and saying, 'But you know Savanna Union Bank has better rates, they sent people to me last week.' Yinka is still smiling and Chioma wonders whether her cheeks are aching. She thinks about the stories in a metal box under her bed. Her father read them all and sometimes he wrote things on the margins: Excellent! Substandard

English! Very good! No imagination! It was he who had bought her novels; her mother thought all she needed were her textbooks. Yinka says, 'Chioma!' and she looks up. The Alhaji is talking to her. He looks almost shy and his eyes do not meet hers. There is a tentativeness towards her that he does not show towards Yinka. 'I am saying you are too fine. Why is it that a Big Man has not married you?' Chioma smiles and says nothing. The Alhaji says, 'I have agreed that I will do business with Merchant Trust but you will be my personal contact,' he said. Chioma smiles, uncertain what to say. 'Of course,' Yinka says. 'She will be your contact. We will take care of you. Ah, thank you sir!' The Alhaji gets up and says, 'Come, come, I have some nice perfumes from my last trip to London. Let me give you something to take home.' He starts to walk inside and then turns. 'Come, come, you two.' Yinka follows. Chioma gets up. The Alhaji turns again to glance at her, to wait for her to follow. But she does not follow. She turns to the door and opens it and walks out into the sparkling sunlight and past the jeep in which the driver is sitting with the door hanging open, listening to the radio. 'Aunty? Aunty, something happen?' he calls. She does not answer. She walks and walks, past the large high gates and keeps walking.

Ujunwa woke up to the crashing sound of the sea, to a nervous clutch in her belly. She did not want to read her story tonight. She did not want to go to breakfast, either, but she went anyway. She said a general 'Good morning' with a general smile. She sat next to the Kenyan and he leaned towards her and whispered that Edward had just told the Senegalese that he had dreamed of her naked navel. Naked navel. Ujunwa watched the Senegalese delicately raising her teacup to her lips, sanguine, looking out at the sea. Ujunwa envied her calm. She felt piqued, too, to hear that Edward was making suggestive remarks to someone else and she wondered what her pique meant. Had she come to see his ogling as her due? She was uncomfortable thinking about this, about reading tonight, and so that afternoon, lingering over lunch, she asked the Senegalese what she had said when Edward spoke of her naked navel.

The Senegalese shrugged and said no matter how many dreams the old man had, she would still remain a lesbian.

'But why do we say nothing?' Ujunwa asked. She raised her voice and looked at the others. 'Why do we always say nothing?'

They looked at each other. The Kenyan told the waiter that the water was getting warm and could he please get some more ice. The Tanzanian asked the waiter where in Malawi he was from. Finally the Zimbabwean said the food at Jumping Monkey Hill was sickening, all that meat and cream. Other words tumbled out and Ujunwa was not sure who said what. Imagine an African gathering with no rice and why should beer be banned at the dinner table just because Edward thought wine was proper and breakfast at eight was too early, never mind that Edward said it was the 'right' time and the smell of his pipe was nauseating and he had to decide which he liked to smoke, anyway, and stop rolling cigarettes halfway through a pipe.

Only the black South African remained silent. He looked bereft, hands clasped in his lap, before he said that Edward was just an old man and meant no harm. Ujunwa shouted to him, 'This kind of attitude is why they could kill you and herd you into townships and require passes from you before you could walk on your own land!' Then she stopped herself and apologized. She should not have said that. She did not mean to raise her voice. The black South African shrugged, as if he understood that the devil would always do his work. The Kenyan was watching Ujunwa. He looked both speculative and surprised. He told her, in a low voice, that she was angry about more than just Edward and she looked away and wondered if 'angry' was the right word.

Later, she went to the souvenir shop with the Kenyan and the Senegalese and tried on jewellery made of faux-ivory. They teased the Kenyan about his interest in jewellery and perhaps he was gay, too? He laughed and said his possibilities were limitless. Then he said, more seriously, that Edward was connected and could find them a London agent; there was no need to antagonize the man, no need to close doors to opportunity. He, for one, didn't want to end at that teacher's job in Nairobi. He was speaking as though to everyone but his eyes were on Ujunwa.

Ujunwa bought a necklace and put it on and liked the look of the white, teeth-shaped pendant against her throat. That evening, Hillary smiled when she saw it. 'I wish people would see how faux-ivory looks real and leave the animals alone,' she said. Ujunwa beamed and said that it was in fact real ivory and wondered whether to add that she had killed the elephant herself during a royal hunt. Hillary looked startled, then pained. Ujunwa fingered the plastic. The cool smoothness was relaxing. She needed to be relaxed, and she said this to herself over and over, as she started to read from her story. Afterward, the Tanzanian said she captured Lagos well, the smells and sounds, and it was incredible how similar Third World cities were. The white South African said she hated that term *Third World* but had loved the realistic portrayal of what women were going through in Nigeria. Edward leaned back and said, 'It's never quite like that in real life, is it? Women are never victims in that sort of crude way and certainly not in Nigeria. Nigeria has women in high positions. The most powerful cabinet minister is a woman.'

The Kenyan cut in and said he liked the story, but didn't believe Chioma would give up the job. This was after all a woman with no other choices, and so he thought the ending was implausible.

'The whole thing is implausible,' Edward said. 'This is agenda writing, it isn't a real story of real people.'

Inside Ujunwa, something shrank. Edward was still speaking. Of course one had to admire the writing itself, which was quite *mah-ve-lous*. He was watching her, and it was the quiet victory in his eyes that made her stand up and start to laugh. The participants stared at her. She laughed and laughed and they watched her and then she picked up her papers. 'The only thing I didn't add in the story,' she said with her eyes on Edward's face, 'is that after I left the Alhaji's house, I got into the jeep and insisted that the driver take me home because I knew it was the last time I would be riding in that car.'

There were other things Ujunwa wanted to say but she did not say them. There were tears crowding up in her eyes but she did not let them out. She was looking forward to calling her mother, and as she walked back to her cabin, she wondered whether this ending, in a story, would be considered plausible. ☐

MAO COMES
TO SYDNEY
Georgia Blain

On the night Gough Whitlam was elected prime minister of Australia in December 1972, my parents held a party at our home in Sydney. It was summer and my mother wore a long Indian kaftan; my father wore a seersucker shirt and casual slacks. My brothers and I were meant to be in bed and watched from upstairs as the grown-ups drank red wine in the courtyard off our kitchen and ate dolmades, Lebanese bread and hummus from plates covered with vine leaves. They cheered loudly when the election results were announced. The country was going to change for the better, my mother told us later. Even my father, who was more conservative, was excited at the prospect of a new leader, someone who would give us our own national identity, he said proudly. The Labor Party was in power for the first time in twenty-three years but we didn't understand the significance of what had occurred. My mother tried to explain that it meant better rights for women, for Aboriginal people; improved health care and education. She needn't have bothered; we were already barracking for Whitlam and his ideals because that is what you did: you went for the party your parents backed.

Soon after the election, the new government established a Royal Commission on Human Relationships and my mother was appointed one of the commissioners. It was a radical change in career from her previous life as a broadcaster. She was already aware of the social divides that existed across the country; she had made radio documentaries that addressed these issues. She was used to fronting up to people, microphone in hand, and getting them to trust her. But as a commissioner, she became completely immersed in the lives of others as she travelled from major cities to tiny outback towns taking evidence. When I asked her what that meant (and I didn't ask her about her work often, I was far too absorbed in my own life), she replied that it was a matter of getting people to talk about themselves. The evidence she heard came from gay men, lesbians, pregnant teenagers, battered wives, women who'd had terminations, parents who had cared for children with disabilities; no one had ever wanted to hear their stories, certainly not the government. It seems amazing to me, in these conservative times, that we once had leaders who genuinely wanted to know how people lived and encouraged them to express their differences. It seems like another country.

In this other country, I went to a new school and what was called
an 'Opportunity Class', which would cater for the needs (whatever
they were) of bright children. It was a half-hour trip away, and on
my first day I travelled there with Timothy, a boy who lived nearby.
He sat next to me on the bus and his voice was loud and boastful.
Did I know we were the smartest children in the state? He flicked
a wad of paper at a woman with Down's syndrome in the seat across
the aisle, giggling as she rubbed at the side of her neck. Timothy
leaned across and whispered 'imbecile' just loud enough for her to
hear. I knew what he was doing was wrong but I was too weak to
stand up to him. I could only shrink away, pressing closer to the
window in an attempt to appear as though I did not know him, until
we finally came to the new school. It was on the highway, a large
cluster of formidable red-brick buildings and cement playgrounds.
Timothy was undaunted and loudly asked everyone if they knew the
way to the Opportunity Class, the one for bright children. He
thanked them cheerfully, oblivious to the sneers of other students.

Mrs Davis was our teacher for the next two years. There were
twenty-five of us and on that first day we all sat on the floor in front
of her. Her slim, athletic legs, which were at our eye level, impressed
me immediately. The rest of her seemed far more ordinary. Her hair
was carefully set in auburn waves. She even wore make-up, bright
chemist colours of which my mother would disapprove. Her frock
was nylon and her sandals were high-heeled. She did not look
unconventional, and yet she insisted to the class that this was what
she was. 'And I expect you to be as well.' We were not the only ones
who had been hand-picked, she told us. She, too, had been selected
for excellence. Her excellence was in teaching, and she was not afraid
of trying out new ideas.

When the moment came for us to tell her, and each other, a little
bit about ourselves, I felt my stomach tighten. The first girl to put
up her hand said her mother was an actor in *Number 96*, the risqué
TV soap of the day. Another girl, Sarah, said her father worked for
Kentucky Fried Chicken; everyone was impressed. Timothy told the
class his father was a judge, Supreme Court in fact, and he tilted his
chin up as he spoke.

I barely listened. I was too anxious about how I would describe
what my mother did. She was a Royal Commissioner, I could say, but

I didn't really know what that meant. She was investigating human relationships, a concept that was just as hard to grasp. Explaining my family would, I feared, mark me out as weird from my very first day. But Mrs Davis clapped her hands. 'Not your parents.' She wanted to know more about us. Why had we decided to come here?

None of us knew how to answer.

Eventually a girl called Melanie put up her hand. 'Because it's an opportunity,' she said, 'to learn.'

'Good,' said Mrs Davis. 'And that is precisely what we will be doing.'

At my old school, I had always done well. Being smart did not bring me any friends. On the contrary, it made me odd, or so I believed. When we did our multiplication tests, I made sure I got a few answers wrong; in English, I misspelled my words on purpose, stumbled over a sentence, or pretended not to understand what a story was about. But now it was different. During that first week in Opportunity Class, I found that my abilities were no longer something to be ashamed about. On the contrary, it was my potential lack of abilities that made me anxious. Now that brains mattered, I was no longer the brightest in the class.

We soon learned that there was a genius among us. Smart enough to go to university already, he had been held back because his parents wanted him to be with children of his own age. 'It's Donovan'—one of the girls pointed to where he sat by himself, eating his lunch as he stared across at the other kids playing. 'He's really good at maths.'

'Georgia is a bohemian,' Timothy declared, dancing in front of me. I protested, although I didn't know what bohemian meant. 'Well, her mother is,' he smirked. 'That's what my dad says. A bohemian and a feminist.'

Sarah, the girl whose father worked for Kentucky Fried Chicken, quickly established herself as the popular girl, the one all the boys liked. Melanie was a leader and was immediately elected to the student council. And then there was Sam. Just as Donovan was our highest benchmark, Sam was the lowest point. He was incapable of paying attention and too fond of distracting others. Mrs Davis would shake her head each time he failed to listen, talked too loudly or uttered a pointless and seemingly stupid remark.

'So, do you like it?' my parents asked me, and now that I have a daughter myself, I know how eager they were to hear that I was happy. As a parent you want to hear your child fits in, she has friends, and she has the courage to be herself. It is hard enough to attain this as an adult. Any honest answer is bound to disappoint. And so I skimped on the details and said I was fine. It wasn't so far from the truth; I was still shy and uncertain about my place in the social hierarchy, but I loved the work.

'We will have privileges,' Mrs Davis told us. The first of these was a state-supplied musical instrument. We could choose from flute, clarinet and oboe and we were to have music lessons every Wednesday afternoon.

We had no sports periods. 'Instead we will exercise each morning,' said Mrs Davis. She was a devotee of the 10BX plan, an exercise programme for an army that would guarantee fitness. She produced a slim dog-eared paperback and showed us diagrams of the routine we would follow. At the end of each exercise session, we had relaxation. One of us was selected to envisage a scenario ('Something that will make your body sink into a dreamlike state,' Mrs Davis explained), while everyone else lay on the floor and listened. I liked being picked for this one. I concocted elaborate stories: a swim in an icy-cold river, lying on a warm boulder with willow trees waving overhead, a flight on a cloud through azure skies, a bed made of silken feathers. I was good at this and, surprisingly, not shy when it came to fantasy.

In the classroom, standard maths, reading and writing were all dismissed as boring. Exercise cards for equations and reading comprehension were stored in a cupboard and only ever used when Mrs Davis was called out or in one of her occasional bad moods. The rest of the time we experimented. We wrote novels, painted murals, cooked exotic foods and put on plays. After years of dull and repetitive learning, this was exciting.

By the end of my first year of Opportunity Class, the Whitlam government was in trouble. During the holidays my mother sat on the edge of our brown woollen armchair watching the news and tried to explain to me what was happening: there had been scandals with members of cabinet, problems with financing ambitious social plans, and it was becoming clear that the conservatives were poised, ready to pounce. But I wasn't really listening; I was too busy writing my latest novel or play.

Despite the news reports, when we returned to the classroom at the start of the new year, Mrs Davis's belief in the great wave of change overtaking the nation was unshaken. She had visited China during the summer: 'As you are probably aware, our Prime Minister, Gough Whitlam, has re-established diplomatic ties with China.'

We all looked at her blankly.

'Does anyone know what this means?'

Only Timothy put up his hand. 'My father thinks Gough Whitlam is a Communist.'

'I am not interested in what your father thinks, Timothy. I am interested in what you think.'

Timothy was not perturbed. 'Communists take away your freedom. Everyone has to be the same. They jail people if they say anything against the government.'

'That's one interpretation,' said Mrs Davis. 'I was enormously privileged to be one of the first group of Westerners allowed into the country. This gave me, shall we say, a vantage point not enjoyed by your father. Communism is about equality. Sharing the wealth.' She wrote the last three words up on the board and underlined them. 'Think of our society.' She turned to face us. 'Some of us are born into money and privilege and it gives us an enormous headstart. Others have to work long, hard days in menial jobs. They will never have much, nor will their children. Communism is about shaking this up. Turning it on its head. Making it fair,' and she leaned forward to emphasize this last word. Timothy had his hand up, but Mrs Davis was ignoring him. 'I was particularly impressed by the ideas behind the Cultural Revolution.' We didn't know what she was talking about. We were middle-class eleven-year-olds on Sydney's suburban Lower North Shore. Communism had not touched our lives.

'The Cultural Revolution was a time of great upheaval. It was a time of challenging every perceived idea and value, of questioning; with the peasants having just as much right, if not more, to question the intellectuals than the intellectuals did to question society.'

She looked at our expressionless faces. 'I would like to try something here in the classroom. An idea that I took away with me. I would like you to rule yourselves.' She waved her hand around the room. 'To come up with your own ideas for solving your own problems. To question what we are doing and to determine solutions that work for you.'

The plan was simple. We were going to form a re-education group. Four of us would be selected by our classmates. The group was to be the funnel through which ideas would go to Mrs Davis. It would also be a forum for other students to air their grievances and problems. It would choose when to meet; it would set up its own rules.

'Who would you like to nominate? Who will be your cadres?'

Melanie was the first to be nominated and seconded, and she accepted the post graciously. Donovan, the genius, was next. Anyone who could do complex algebra and logarithms could surely solve the problems of an eleven-year-old. *Pick me, pick me*, I thought. I knew I was in with a chance; I had made a real effort to seem sensible, good and nice—it was a new act that I was trying on, one that I would continue to refine for many years—and it paid off. Jason, a bright-eyed boy with endless energy and enthusiasm, was the last to be selected.

We held our first meeting straight away while the rest of the class continued with their lesson. 'If there is a problem you feel you cannot deal with, you must call on me,' Mrs Davis told us. We all nodded in mute understanding.

As she turned to leave, Jason voiced what we had all been wondering. 'So what is it that we are meant to be doing?'

Thankfully we had Melanie. With her long blonde hair neatly brushed into two pigtails and a school uniform that was always clean and ironed, she never looked less than perfect, but it was her certainty that I envied most. She was always the first to put her hand up, the first to volunteer. 'I think we should discuss whether there's anything we would like to change,' she suggested.

It seemed ridiculous that we could have any real power. Surely no one was actually going to listen to us? We didn't really know what we wanted, so we confined ourselves to small things: perhaps a few more excursions, the odd film at lunch time?

Just as we were about to call the meeting to a close, there was a knock on the door and we looked at each other, surprised. If it had seemed ludicrous to think that we could make suggestions about our education, it seemed even more ridiculous that anyone in the class would actually want to talk to us. But it appeared someone did.

Shane came in and sat nervously in the spare seat that made up our circle, looking down at the ground as we asked him what he wanted to discuss. Scratching the top of his knee, eyes still fixed on the floor, he eventually told us it was his projects. 'I can't get them finished on time.' His voice was so soft I had to lean forward.

'Is it because you find the work difficult?' Donovan asked.

Shane shook his head. After his mum had left, he had to help his dad every night. By the time he'd made dinner and got his younger brothers to bed, he was just too tired to do his schoolwork. None of us had known that Shane didn't have a mum. I knew single-parent families existed, but no one ever spoke about them. Melanie looked concerned as she asked him whether he missed his mother. I turned to look at her, wondering if she was as grown-up as she seemed or just very good at pretending.

Shane shrugged.

'Have you talked to your dad about this?' Melanie asked.

He shrugged again. His dad didn't get home until eight. He had to make the dinner.

'Maybe you could get a housekeeper,' I suggested. We had one. I wanted to be helpful like the others.

Shane didn't even look at me.

Melanie took charge again. She thanked Shane for talking to us and said that it would be best if we discussed this alone. We would call him back and let him know what we thought.

'God, imagine not having a mother,' she said after he left. Her huge blue eyes welled up with tears. 'Now I feel terrible I didn't ask him to my birthday.'

'I think we should tell him to talk to Mrs Davis,' Donovan suggested. We called Shane back in. He scratched at a scab on his elbow, not looking up as Melanie delivered our verdict.

When I told my parents about the group, I don't think they really understood what it was, or what the approval of my peers meant to me. But it wasn't just my parents who didn't understand what we were doing; I'm not sure that we did, either. Mrs Davis thought the group was important and that was enough to give us (Melanie and me in particular) a certain smugness about our new position. We used secrecy to reinforce our status, rarely talking about our meetings with anyone else in the class, no matter how ordinary the problems we discussed. After our encounter with Shane, the dilemmas we were asked to resolve were trivial: they ranged from what to wear to a birthday party to how to make sure all the good books hadn't been taken out of the library before our class had its turn.

Genuine requests for help were rare and the number of students who came to see us began to dwindle. Melanie and Jason gossiped during our meetings, while Donovan and I tried to make conversation. So we were surprised when Melanie called an urgent meeting.

Sarah knocked on the door. 'I want you to do something about Sam. He keeps trying to kiss me.' She grimaced. 'And I'm not the only one.' Melanie confirmed her best friend's complaint. 'He's done it to a few of us. It's disgusting.'

The rest of us didn't know what to say. 'Does he know you don't like it?' I asked feebly, knowing that she and some of the other girls played spin the bottle at lunch.

Sarah rolled her eyes. 'What do you reckon?'

Jason, who sometimes played with Sam, looked the most uncomfortable. 'I don't really know if we can talk to him. I mean, what do we say? Why would he listen to us?'

Donovan reminded us that Mrs Davis had always said she would be there to help us if a problem was too difficult for us to deal with alone, and as soon as he spoke, we all latched on to the idea with relief. She came immediately, sitting down in the circle and telling us we were absolutely right to call on her if we needed her, she would do what she could, and she looked around the room, her gaze stopping on Sarah. 'Perhaps it would be best if you explained what's been happening.'

Sarah's assurance vanished. 'It's just Sam,' she eventually said. 'He kisses us—the girls, that is—and we don't like it.'

'It's true,' Melanie added. 'It's happened to a few of us.'

Mrs Davis tapped her frosted pink nails on the armrest of her chair. We wondered whether she was cross with us for wasting her time, but she quickly put our doubts to rest. 'This is indeed a serious problem.' She stood up and began to pace the room. 'I'm very glad you called me.' Her vehemence surprised me. Sam's actions didn't seem to deserve it. 'Georgia,' she said, 'I want you to go and call Sam in. I will speak to him now.'

The classroom was noisy. Everyone was taking advantage of Mrs Davis being out of the room. They stopped as soon as I opened the door and then continued when they saw it was only me. Sam was flicking elastic bands at another boy. 'Sam,' I said, my voice too soft. I had to say his name again before he turned in my direction, grinning. 'You have to come with me. To the re-education group.'

'What for?' The grin was still there, but his eyes darted quickly from me to the door.

'We just need to speak to you.'

As he followed me out, I heard Timothy snicker: 'She won't pash you—she's frigid.' My cheeks burned. I hated him.

Sam stood in the entrance of our meeting room, looking nervous.

'Sit down,' Mrs Davis commanded. 'I have heard some very serious allegations.' She paused. 'And I am deeply distressed.'

Sam was white. I dared glance at him only once and quickly looked away before there was any chance of catching his eye. 'You have been making unwanted sexual advances towards the girls in this class.' She sat upright as she pointed her finger at him. 'And I would like to hear your response.'

'I haven't.' He looked up and squirmed in his chair, unable to do anything but deny the accusation.

'That's not what I've been told. Your behaviour has been the cause of several complaints and, quite frankly, I see no reason not to believe them.'

'But I didn't do it.' The words caught in the back of his throat.

'You did,' Sarah said. 'You've done it to me, and Melanie and Louise. You know you have.'

Sam told her it was just a joke, she knew it was. 'Besides, you kiss people. You play spin the bottle.'

Mrs Davis turned to Sarah.

'In the classroom, at lunch time.'

'That's not true.' Sarah's face was red. Mrs Davis looked at Melanie, who confirmed her friend's lie.

But Mrs Davis was once again focused on Sam. 'How dare you treat this as a joke?' In the silence that followed, Sam sat back in his chair, his body now limp. 'Do you know what will become of you?' He shook his head, he was crying.

'You will be a rapist. Do you know what a rapist is?'

He shook his head again.

'It is a man who forces himself upon women.'

He sniffed loudly.

'And that is precisely what you have been doing.'

He opened his mouth to speak but no words came out.

'And do you know what happens to rapists?'

He didn't.

'They go to jail.'

Mrs Davis stared at him for a moment. 'You will stand out in the corridor for the rest of the afternoon, and if anyone asks why you are there, you will tell them. Say it.'

'I am here so that I will not be a rapist.' We could hardly hear him and his nose was running with snot.

'Now get out of my sight.'

Sam shut the door behind him and Mrs Davis came back to her seat. She sighed heavily. She had to save him from himself, from a future in prison, she told us. We had been wise and responsible in bringing the matter to her. She hoped she would never have to deal with anything like that again. We all filed out of the room. We could see Sam standing alone at the end of the hall but didn't look at him directly.

We held only one more meeting of the re-education group. Donovan said that he didn't see much point in continuing. Students weren't asking to see us, and he was tired of missing out on lessons. Exams for selective high-school entrance were looming; we all agreed. Melanie explained our decision to Mrs Davis, who seemed to understand. The experiment had worked well. We could always re-form if there was a call for our services again. She thanked us all for the responsible job we had done and took us back to class. She clapped her hands for silence. 'Unless there are any objections to the contrary, the re-education group has informed me that it will, for the moment, cease to exist. I'm sure you would like to thank the members, your cadres, for the role they have played in creating a harmonious environment.' As we stood in front of the class, my eyes met Sam's for one brief moment. Quickly I looked away.

My mother went on writing her report for the Royal Commission. After the dismissal of the Whitlam government in 1975, the commissioners had been ordered to wind up their work and many of the staff, my mother included, wrote their sections from home. When the report's findings were leaked to the press, newspaper articles referred to it as a 'sick and misguided document' influenced by 'the deviant lobby', warning that children would be having sex and getting abortions, and that every parent in Australia should oppose its recommendations. Strangers spat on my mother as we waited in supermarket queues. I couldn't understand how they could tell her she had no morals and shouldn't be bringing up children. My mother was angry, but not just on her own behalf. She explained that the people who had come to speak to the commissioners had been brave. She felt they had been let down.

Half listening, I dismissed her talk as adult. After all, it was only politics, and I was too young to understand. □

THE POETRY SOCIETY

Poems of Identity

in a changing world

The Poetry Society presents a pre-National
Poetry Day reading on the theme of *Identity*
by **Moniza Alvi, Simon Armitage,
Jackie Kay** and **Nick Laird**.
Hosted by **Joan Bakewell**.

Thursday 28 September at 7.30pm
St Giles-in-the-Fields Church, 60 St Giles High Street,
London, WC2H 8LG

Tickets: £10 / £5 Poetry Society members and concs.
Bookings: 020 7420 9895

www.nationalpoetryday.org.uk

THE POETRY SOCIETY

IMAGE © ISTOCKPHOTO.COM/ALEX BRAMMELL

SOCIETY OF AUTHORS

The Society of Authors
Grants

The Society is offering grants to published
authors who need funding to assist in the
writing of their next book. Writers of fiction,
non-fiction and poetry may apply. The grants
are provided by the Authors' Foundation and
the K. Blundell Trust.

Closing date: 30 September 2006

Full details from:

website: www.societyofauthors.org
email: info@societyofauthors.org

or send an SAE to
The Awards Secretary, The Society of
Authors, 84 Drayton Gardens,
London SW10 9SB.

TWINS
Jeremy Seabrook

Jeremy Seabrook (left) and his twin

My twin brother and I were separated at birth, even though we lived in the same house, with the same mother, for the first eighteen years of our lives. The separation was total, psychological, emotional and social; and it lasted until his death early in 2005. I heard only indirectly that he had died, since there had been no communication between us since our mother's funeral, fifteen years earlier.

I can scarcely believe these words, even as I write them. How could we have grown up in such intense physical closeness, and yet behave towards each other as though we were strangers? It was worse than being strangers, for we had been familiar everyday figures in each other's life. There was a deep temperamental difference between us; but this was reinforced by the determination of a powerful woman, and by a social system that supported separation. Our mother had skilfully maintained the state of hostile indifference that kept us apart; and we lived together in a state of frozen kinship, our lives both turned towards our mother. Our relationship—or absence of one—was decided from the beginning.

Or maybe even before that. When our mother was already well into her thirties and still childless, she discovered that her husband had tertiary syphilis. He had always been a 'wanderer', a characteristic that referred as much to his sexual rovings as to his need for constant physical movement. My earliest memories of him are of watching as he shaved himself in readiness for an evening out, scraping his neck with a cut-throat razor and plastering his curly black hair with lard to make it shine. The symptoms of syphilis were attributed for a long time to an infection contracted while catching rabbits—he was also an accomplished poacher, and at one time kept a ferret in a hutch in the garden.

Our mother had already had a series of miscarriages. The treatment for syphilis in the late 1930s involved continuous injections of a mixture of mercury and arsenic, and there was little prospect that sexual relations between them would ever resume, and even less that they would have any children.

She was standing one day at the kitchen window which looked on to a piece of waste ground, when a man working on a nearby building site asked for a bucket of water. He came into the kitchen to collect it. She immediately saw that he was no ordinary workman:

this was a time when the working class was full of earnest self-taught people, autodidacts, the intelligent uninstructed and people hungry for knowledge. Our town, Northampton, had its good share of them. Within a few minutes, he had promised to lend her some books— George Bernard Shaw's *The Intelligent Woman's Guide to Socialism*, William Morris's *News from Nowhere* and Robert Blatchford's *Merrie England*. I found them among her small treasures after her death.

She must have decided there and then that he would become the father of the child she so much wanted. She could scarcely believe her good fortune. He was everything her husband was not: clever, smart and in perfect health. Although he was married, he made it clear he had no intention of leaving his wife. They had no children. She was a semi-invalid. Discovery, he said, would destroy her. The relationship between them developed quickly. Within months she was pregnant.

Dealing with this was no simple matter. Appalled and elated by what she had done, she came to an accommodation with her husband. She was by then looking after the butcher's shop they had taken on a new housing estate, while nursing a man whose shaming illness would certainly have ruined the family livelihood if it had become known. It was wartime. She promised that she would look after him until he was fully recovered, and then she expected him to be gone. In the meantime, he would accept that the child she was carrying was his. He had no choice. When she was not serving in the shop, she was emptying zinc pails of waste discharged from his mouth and nose, which had been partly destroyed by the sickness. She always said that the stench remained with her for the rest of her life. She used quantities of bleach and disinfectant, which she travelled far afield to buy, lest anyone should wonder why she needed so much of a commodity which did not figure prominently in most people's weekly shopping list.

He fiercely resented his dependency, and there were frequent arguments. I remember standing at the top of the stairs early one morning and watching as he threw a cup of tea at her: it flew solid through the air before shattering in scalding drops on her face and shoulder. Frightened by what he had done, he burst into tears. He was in more urgent need of consolation than she was of medical attention, and she administered it, despite her injuries. Sometimes she would pretend to be hurt by his clumsy blows and would lie still on the floor. He would panic and try to revive her. I saw her often, prone, in a posture that prefigured my worst nightmare.

As it turned out, she was to have twins as a result of this encounter with a stranger. Here was a tangle of secrets to be concealed at all costs. Was it her own secretiveness that made her insist her children tell her everything, keep nothing back? Sometimes she would say, 'There's nothing I don't know,' and she turned upon us her grim grey eyes, in which we saw reflected our own guilt and shame. We yielded up to her everything she asked for, including a promise that we would never desert her as others had. She extracted from her children promises of constancy which the men in her life had withheld.

Her main concern was to keep the two men apart, and to ensure they would never meet. Our biological father, aggrieved at what he saw as her trickery, refused to contribute anything to our upkeep. Who can tell what menacing possibility she foresaw if her twin boys should combine or conspire against her, when one man had deserted her for a sexually transmitted disease and the other had abandoned her to the consequences of what he called her own lack of foresight?

I don't think any meeting between our joint fathers ever did occur; just as no significant encounter between their divided children ever took place. Later, as we grew up, our 'true' father occasionally made an appearance in our lives; unaccountably lachrymose and emotional, he questioned us closely about our ambitions and what we wanted to be when we grew up, a state so unimaginably distant at the time that it was difficult to formulate any answer at all. We resented his intrusive enquiries. It seems he was angered by her deception and, repelled by the role he had been selected to play, felt manipulated and abused: it had not been for his own sake that our mother had been attracted to him, but for the sake of as yet unknown others, her future children. He made it clear she could expect no material help; and even when she could scarcely make a living in the late 1940s, as the meat ration fell to the equivalent of 10d a person, she didn't ask him for anything. She was frugal and sparing, and spent nothing on herself, while we had what she emphatically called 'the best of everything'. Nothing was too good for us, except the one thing we might have valued above all else, the sweetness of uninhibited companionship.

As soon as her husband was well—by that time we were eight or nine—they were divorced. Divorce, despite being a rare occurrence, was the inevitable outcome of the one-sided bargain she had struck with him; and separation was an art in which she was already practised. Some virtuous people in the neighbourhood ostentatiously withdrew their ration book from the shop: who could be expected to deal with tradespeople who had flouted the sacrament of marriage? She accepted their judgement with dignity, thankful that nobody knew the whole story. At the same time, certain men propositioned her. They must have been discouraged by her response.

The effort and energy she spent on ensuring that my brother and I grew up as distant from each other as possible were relentless. She watched us all the time. One day, when we were about four, we were giggling in a corner over some trivial amusement. She parted us roughly. We were puzzled by her anger. Significantly, she told me to go and look at a book, and my brother to play with the dog.

The distribution of roles had already long been made. We were physically and psychically isolated. I was clever and he was beautiful: no more malign division could be imagined. It was decided that I would rise socially and he would break hearts. The emotional causes of my estrangement from my brother were woven into our mother's psychological fears; but they were also strengthened and reinforced by circumstances which, in the 1950s, made it possible for my brother and me to be assigned to different social classes, a fact which has continued to bewilder and pain me every day of my life, and never more so than now that he is dead.

The separation was made easier by the fact that our characters and temperaments could not have been less compatible. All we had in common was a shared introversion, and this made communication between us even more difficult.

He slept in a room of his own from the age of about six. I continued to share a room with my mother, frightened, as I was, of the dark, of shadows, of death. My mother's husband, the man we called our father, had been consigned to 'the spare room', a damp and prohibited chamber, which smelled of smoke and rancidity, the unspoken mingling of maleness with disease. It exercised its own fateful lure, and sometimes I would cast a fearful glance at the disorder within—the dingy bedclothes folded back to reveal the mysterious hollow in which his body slept, the blot of mildew on the damp wall, the smell of semen, all of which combined to furnish me with early fantasies of the stranger who represented the absent intimacy of fatherhood. I had erotic dreams about him, which induced a further, and wholly unnecessary, sense of guilt, since in the end he proved to have been no blood relation at all. All this led to a profound estrangement from my own gender.

Our mother rigorously policed the slow unfolding of our maleness, which she would have preferred us to abjure. One day, when I was about nine, undressing in front of the fire, where we had our night-time strip-down wash, she inspected my underpants. I had dribbled into them after peeing. She sniffed and looked up me suspiciously. 'What's this?' I was terrified. 'Wee-wee. What else could it be?' She examined the stained garment dubiously. 'What else could it be?' 'Never you mind.' I kept on asking—and wondering—what it could have signified. 'What else could it be?' This served as a premature and elliptical form of sex instruction: I concluded that other, and no doubt shameful, discharges might in time be expected from my body. Our childhood was pervaded by her mute entreaty that, if time rendered adulthood inevitable, we should at least not grow up to be men. This had a seriously repressive effect on my brother, whose emotional and sexual development was delayed by her mute prohibitive power; whereas I tried to oblige, although the best I could do was to grow up gay.

There was no space for emotional attachment to my brother. Our mother whispered to each of us her dissatisfaction with the other, with the consequence that we viewed one another with distrust and a fierce defensiveness of our wronged parent.

Separation has been, perhaps, the single biggest determining influence in my life. The completeness of separation from my twin was accompanied by a morbid fear of separation from my mother. For the first few years of my life, I could not bear to lose sight of her; whenever she was swallowed up by the closing of a door or even by extinguishing the light, I howled until her presence was restored to me. It seems that the premature loss of my brother was accompanied by an excessive attachment to her: she was, as it were, the phantom of a kind of amputation of the twin who was always present but scarcely visible.

My dependency on our mother, and my terror of losing her, set up other pathologies. Her departure (or death, which seemed a more likely agent of her disappearance) seemed to me the most terrible thing that could happen; and I came early to the comfortless conclusion that it would be folly ever to permit myself the pain of any other relationship which would involve the same frightening abridgement. For this reason, all my feelings (and not only those of love) were locked up in the claustral relationship with her, and I was unwilling to form—or perhaps incapable of—any other close attachment, least of all with the brother whose extinguished presence remained as inert to me as that of the kitchen table or the contents of the broom cupboard.

For a long time, I did not recognize the origin of what later appeared to me an inability to feel for others. I took refuge in dwelling upon the suffering of humanity in general, the brevity of life, the certainty of death, but this was the only way I could express the stifled emotions of a dependency that had little to do with love, but everything to do with the fear of loss. I was well into my thirties before I knew the meaning of a reciprocal and loving relationship with another adult. I didn't reason it like this, but I felt that since irreparable loss is inscribed in every relationship, I should stay away from them. And I did.

I think my brother may have experienced something similar; indeed, it may well have been worse for him, since he did not so readily yield to our mother's demand for unconditional surrender to her will. I had the misfortune to resemble her. He didn't, and this is why he probably felt the exercise of her controlling power as violence. She could not tie him to herself as she had effortlessly bound me. As a result, she made greater efforts to attach him, which he found intolerably oppressive. This led him to believe that she cared more for me than for him, and only I knew that the opposite was the truth. I was a pushover, while he was a challenge. Her attempts to win him over were evidence of a preference which he could not, perhaps, have been expected to see. I was jealous of his difference, and of his ability to resist, which suggested an independence I wanted. I had little sympathy for him, and nothing remained in the depleted account of my feelings to spend on him.

I can now see the many ways in which I failed him, although at the time these remained opaque and mysterious to me. One day in primary school, he fell ill and had to be taken home. I begged that someone else might go with him, since I did not wish to miss the lesson. I remember feeling virtuous in making this request, and if the teacher gave me a strange look of pity and puzzlement, its meaning became clear to me only much later. On another occasion, walking home from school, he had what was politely called 'an accident': suffering from diarrhoea, he stood immobile on the path, his legs stained with shit. Appalled, I abandoned him and ran home to tell our mother what had happened. She closed the shop and went out to meet him. Gathering some dock leaves from the hedgerow, she wiped him down and brought him back, consoling him with the story that, although I had fled the scene of his embarrassment and shame, he could trust her never to do so.

I was convinced that my brother brought nothing but trouble and unhappiness to her. That, presumably, was why she never ceased worrying about him and chose me as her confidant. On the day her own mother died, in November 1948, I was in bed with one of the unnamed sicknesses that impaired my childhood. She came upstairs and leaned over the bed, her eyes dark and her cheeks smeared with tears. 'What's the matter?' I asked. 'Is it him?' To my brother, in order to explain her yielding to the constant demands I made on her, she used to say, 'Well, you know what he is', so that he also came to understand that I was the source of her constant suffering. She had developed a complicity with each of us against the other, and she betrayed us all the time, in order to prevent us from betraying her.

But all this careful engineering of our souls was moved by an overwhelming and expiatory love. She felt guilty that she had brought two illegitimate children into the world at a time when such children still bore the stigma of events over which they had not the slightest influence. Enough people were in on the secret for its inevitable disclosure at some point. The wounds were inflicted by the most tender hands, and these are always more painful than those delivered with the intention of hurting. The work of separation was not conscious, and if anyone had pointed out what she was doing, she would have been appalled. The most anyone ever said was, 'They are like chalk and cheese'; which of these substances each of us resembled was not spoken.

She needn't have taken quite so much trouble to keep us apart. The social arrangements which would assist her so ably in her work of separation were at hand. At eleven, he went to the secondary modern school, which was a scruffy holding centre for the wayward youngsters of an estate known as Windy Ridge, into which former town centre slum-dwellers had been transferred. I had gone prematurely, at the age of ten, to the grammar school. While he struggled in the C-stream (against teachers, the other kids and low expectations), I raced through my studies, and soon learned to ascribe to myself all the qualities which a new meritocracy claimed to have detected in me. My brother was said to be 'good with his hands'; but everyone knew that was a euphemism for not being a scholar, and was in fact a humiliating consolation prize. He came home with objects he had crafted—a wooden stool, a small chest of drawers—on which he had concentrated all his considerable creative powers; our mother kept the little chest beside her chair for the rest of her life. It became a small shrine to him; and when she died we found it contained some of his rare letters to her from his time in the army in Germany, his wedding photographs and pictures of his children as infants.

Largely self-taught, she retained a veneration for formal education; and my brother's inability to conform to her superstition, created one of the most significant rifts between us. She also sought, not very successfully, to cultivate in us a taste for the arts as she understood them, in her obscure yearning for a better life that went beyond the material. This meant being allowed to stay up late on Sunday evenings to listen to a concert of light classics on the radio, called *Grand Hotel*, which featured the singing voices of Margaret Eaves and Olive Groves, singing from *The Merry Widow* or *White Horse Inn*. She read to us from her favourite book, *Bleak House*. The first part about the fog was entrancing; but when it came to Lady Dedlock and the incessant rain in Lincolnshire, I was frightened: perhaps it evoked too sharply the narrow, oppressive horizons of our own lives. I wept so much that the readings had to be suspended. They never resumed.

My brother left school at fifteen to be apprenticed to a carpenter and joiner. He came home shedding pale wood shavings and the resinous scent of distant pine forests. He would go out of the house every morning on his bicycle, with a tin box of sandwiches and an apple, skidding in the icy February dawn, while I remained in bed, anticipating further adventures in the subjunctive of French verbs. He worked diligently and uncomplainingly, although once, when he had been detained for prolonged and unpaid overtime, our mother went up to workshop and told his boss that if he thought he could exploit a boy because he had no father who would stand up for him, he had another think coming, because she was as capable as any man at defending him. In fact, she often said to us that she had had to be both father and mother to us, and I sometimes wondered at the effortless capacity with which she could pass in and out of genders, when I had such difficulty in establishing a security in just one of them.

In his spare time, my brother used to make model aeroplanes with balsa wood, covered with tissue paper and stuck together with a glue that smelled of molten bone, and which had the effect of inducing a euphoria which no one at that time could quite identify.

As an adolescent, he went out regularly for Sunday evening cycle rides with Uncle Alex, husband of my mother's eldest sister. He was a gaunt, taciturn man, dominated by his wastrel wife, whose fondness for whisky, melodrama and horse-racing scandalized her family. He took my brother to visit country churches, admiring medieval misericords and vestigial wall-paintings. They would drink lemonade outside pubs, to the melancholy accompaniment of church bells and acrid October bonfires. I was always incredulous at this unlikely friendship, which had so small a dependency on words; perhaps there was a tacit understanding that both were victims of the powerful women of our mother's family. I once came across Alex with our mother, she all flustered and blushing, he saying, 'You're the one I should have had.' It later emerged that he had worked his way through the sisters and had had a relationship with at least two of the others, excluding the one to whom he was officially wedded. It occurred to me that if he was so assiduous in seeking out the lustreless company of my brother, this was probably a pretext which would open up the way to our mother; and I felt obscurely comforted by the realization.

Once my brother tried to talk to me about sex. Although by then—we were about fifteen—I knew much about the mechanics of sex, I could not conceive of sharing with him either what I knew or what I suspected about myself. When I consider our time together, I am aware that during our childhood and youth he made a number of oblique pleas to me. If I rebuffed them, it was because I had no idea of what they were, and regarded them as trespass or encroachment on the slender areas of autonomy remaining to me after our mother had, like some imperial power, annexed all the emotional territory around her, which she governed like the empress-queen herself.

At eighteen, he was 'called up' into the army; significant verb— he had been called up by others all his life. Indeed, our very birth had been a summons from our mother to relieve her of her own isolation and despair. He was posted to Germany, while I remained in the sixth form, acting with my friends in plays in the Co-op Hall, and discussing the iniquities of Suez and the Hungarian uprising against the Soviet Union. I took it as no more than due recognition that I would go to Cambridge, deferring indefinitely a military service which had been abolished by the time I had finished my prolonged and indispensable studies into the symbolism of the celestial rose in Dante's *Paradiso*.

I envied him his looks. My schoolfriends found my brother fascinating, and were often attracted, in ways which they could not then satisfactorily explain to themselves, to his silent beauty. He exercised a mysterious power to draw people to him, which I certainly did not possess. This irritated me, since it suggested that my public proclaimed supremacy might be less significant than I imagined. If he coveted that which came to me so easily, I was bitterly resentful of that which he had never earned. How little we value what we do without effort or merit; and how we long for what is not granted to us! In any case, I was probably quite wrong to be jealous of my brother's attractiveness. Since a great deal of his charm lay in his artless unconsciousness of it, it was of no use to him, and he failed to employ it in the knowing way I would have done, had I been so favoured.

My own apparent good fortune was not without its problems. Life at the grammar school was frightening and I stayed away as much as I could, even writing notes to the headmaster from our departed father, excusing my frequent truancies. One teacher, a lay preacher who had some notion of pastoral care of the pupils, visited our house one day to look into the reasons for my constant absences. When he saw my brother, he turned to me and said, 'Why didn't you tell me you had such a lovely brother?' and playfully let his hand roam over his thigh. I was outraged by his question: I was, after all, the object of his visit, and the question struck me as an accusation, as though I had locked my brother away or concealed his existence from those who would have been only too delighted to learn of it. Far from revealing the cause of my loathing of school, I clenched inside, determined that I would never disclose any feeling or thought to this insensitive man, with his wheedling tone and wandering hands.

There were rare occasions on which my brother and I went out together. I can recall a day one summer holiday, when we walked our aunt's dog through the fields on a thundery afternoon, when huge anvil clouds blotted the sun and the rain began to fall, scenting like caramel the burnt grasses. Nothing happened: only that I caught a glimpse of the companionability we might have had together, and of the confidences we might have shared. The day remains, saturated with rain and regret.

Later—I remember the date, August 1, 1958, a rare day of warmth in a cold, wet summer—we went to the theatre in London. It was a performance of an Australian play called *The Summer of the Seventeenth Doll*, about a group of people who met each summer to reaffirm their friendships and marriages; but in the seventeenth year of their celebration, everything went wrong and they quarrelled irretrievably. He was enchanted by it. Afterwards, we went for a meal in a dismal one-storey fish restaurant on Tottenham Court Road, where, after reading the menu, he asked for 'steak and chips'. I corrected him. 'He means skate and chips,' I told the waiter, as though I were the child of an immigrant, interpreting for a parent who had never mastered the language.

After national service, my brother worked in the construction industry, helping to reshape the face of our town, transforming its ornamental blood-red brick into pale geometric structures of concrete and glass. He worked for the local council as assistant supervisor on the building of the first multi-storey car park—a dazzling symbol of modernity, evidence that our town had indeed entered the modern era. At the same time, I was lamenting the passing of the streets which were being torn down with such exuberance—yet another curious division of labour between us. He represented the future, while I was drawn to the past. While he looked to the age of concrete and cars, I was organizing protests against the construction of an expressway, which would demolish almost a thousand houses, the 'little palaces', as people called the terraced houses they had bought and tended with such care. This further separation was to have fateful results: it was a direct contributor to his early death.

He was, of course, also called to get married. His marriage was arranged; not in the way that matchmakers and extended families in India make marriages, but through the more or less inevitable acceptance of decent people that this was the natural order of things, that they were made for each other, the silent handsome man and the homely and dutiful young woman who wrote to him every day while he was in Germany.

It proved to be a sad error, in which the naivety of the protagonists and the eagerness of the families combined to create a marriage which only kindled the smothered dissatisfactions and the deep inner misery that childhood and adolescence had deposited, tenacious as limescale, on the interior of his trusting and receptive soul. He once spoke, in one rare confessional moment, of being buried alive.

He went to work in Zambia, and there met the woman who was to become his second wife. It was only with her that he began to discover himself, and was able to determine who he was and what he needed. She gave him the confidence and strength he had never received from anyone in the long years of denial. He was already over thirty. His second marriage was a rebirth. Unhappily, this also meant the death of his former self, that inauthentic shell made up of duty, obedience and self-effacement, and of all who had been involved in its making. He detached himself from everyone and everything that had gone before, with the obduracy of those whose will has always been thwarted by others.

He literally remade himself, and in the process discarded his birth family and everyone connected with it. The rift which had run through our childhood, reinforced by our upbringing as effectively as if we had lived under some stringent laws of an emotional apartheid, became final. A few clumsy gestures at reconciliation, an occasional meeting full of suppressed anger and unspoken resentment, brought us to an intractable estrangement which nothing, it seemed, had the power to dissolve.

He came to our mother's funeral, although he had not seen her for some years. I held out my hand to him. He said, 'I'll shake your hand and that's it.' Those were the last words I heard him say. I knew I would never speak to him again. After that, I grieved for him. I woke in the night, unable to believe that this was how our sombre and unsparing childhood, gravid with secrets and sorrows which our mother had confided only when we were almost forty and the two men in her life were dead, would end. Adulthood is always full of mysterious secrets for children: when these are compounded with shame, guilt and remorse with no obvious cause, they can become virulently destructive. Children will inevitably assume that they are at the centre of what is being concealed; and in this case, we were not mistaken. Our mother thought she was sheltering us from harm; but she sought to protect us with her own hurt and wounded feelings—the very source of the damage from which she would have shielded us. Sometimes she could not prevent herself from saying, 'If only you knew.' 'If only we knew what, Mum?' 'Never you mind.' Or, 'You'll know one day.'

As the years passed, I thought about my brother less often; but there remained a dull ache, a sense of absence, the phantom limb of an amputee. When I received the news that he had died, it was like confirmation that the body of a missing person had been found after a long search. He had vanished fifteen years earlier, and the remains washed up on the shore of the time that divided us were identified as his.

There was another bitter irony in his death. He died of mesothelioma, an asbestos-related cancer. This was a consequence of his building work, which had produced multi-storey car parks and concrete office blocks in our town, and also, no doubt, in Lusaka and Windhoek, where he worked, supplied with the miracle substance that was to make them proof against fire. His early working-class occupation also determined his premature death. Although he had appeared as an emissary of the future, altering the aspect of Victorian and colonial towns and cities, the past was not to release him so readily.

Over time, the class destination of our early years was transformed. The separation ceased to be so clearly based on class and mutated, so that it later came to appear that the distance was culturally rather than class-determined. He was dedicated to his family and his work, was prosperous and certainly at peace in the life he led in a converted parsonage in the west of England. I had fulfilled my mother's ambition and become a writer, an occupation which my brother held in the greatest contempt. Our mother came to agree with him: it never pleased her that I wrote about poor people. Nobody, she predicted—quite correctly—wanted to know about that. Had she not sacrificed herself, so that we should be sheltered against the asperities of poverty? Why would I return to such things, if not out of perverseness, in order to humiliate her and mock all her efforts on our behalf? Nothing would come of it. She prided herself on her capacity for prophecy, and although she was shown to be conspicuously fallible in most of her forecasts, in this she was right.

The man we did not know was our father also contributed to the differences between us—a practical demonstration of the power of heredity, since neither of us had the faintest idea of his role in our lives until our mother's belated disclosure. He had been a craftsman, a builder, and a restorer of churches and historic buildings, and my brother had inherited his ability to mend and remake beautiful things. He had also been a vehement Leftist, and a member of the Communist Party, as some of his books remaining with our mother testified. From him, I received a hatred of the orthodoxies of the age, a compulsive dissent from all the revealed ideologies and received wisdom that seem to be indispensable for social cohesion.

George Eliot once wrote of Nature as 'a great tragic dramatist' that unites people by flesh and bone and then divides them by temperament and character. The sensibility that set me apart from my brother was supported by a social system that emphasized competitiveness, disunity and division; the dislocations of kinship were aggravated by social circumstances. That after an unhappy childhood and youth my brother found himself content at last is a consolation; that we were never able to reach out in reconciliation means that death has become one more, and final, aspect of the multiple injuries of separation that dominated our lives.   □

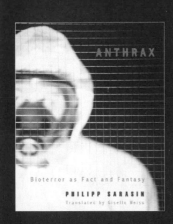

SAFE
Claire Keegan

When sunlight reaches the foot of the dressing table, you get up and look through the suitcase again. It's hot in New York but it may turn cold in winter. All morning the bantam cocks have crowed. It's not something you will miss. You must dress and wash, polish your shoes. Outside, dew lies on the fields, white and blank as pages. Soon the sun will burn it off. It's a fine day for the hay.

In her bedroom your mother is moving things around, opening and closing doors. You wonder what it will be like for her when you leave. Part of you doesn't care. She talks through the door: 'You'll have a boiled egg?'

'No thanks, Ma.'

'You'll have something?'

'Later on, maybe.'

'I'll put one on for you.'

Downstairs, water spills into the kettle, the bolt slides back. You hear the dogs rush in, the shutters folding. You've always preferred this house in summer: the cool feeling in the kitchen, the back door open, scent of the dark wallflowers after rain.

In the bathroom you brush your teeth. The screws in the mirror have rusted, and the glass is cloudy. You look at yourself and know you have failed the Leaving Cert. The last exam was history and you blanked out on the dates. You confused the methods of warfare, the kings. English was worse. You tried to explain that line about knowing the dancer from the dance.

In the bedroom you take out the passport. You look sad in the photograph, lost. The ticket says you will arrive in Kennedy Airport at 12.25. You will be flying against time. You take one last look around the room: walls papered yellow with roses, high ceiling stained where the slate came off, cord of the electric heater swinging out like a tail from under the bed. It used to be an open room at the top of the stairs but Eugene put an end to all of that, got the carpenters in and the partition built, installed the door. You remember him giving you the key, how much that meant to you at the time.

Downstairs, your mother stands over the gas cooker waiting for the pot to boil. You stand at the door and look out. It hasn't rained for days; the spout that runs down from the yard is little more than a trickle. The scent of hay drifts up from neighbouring fields. As soon as the dew burns off, the Rudd brothers will be out in the meadows turning the rows, saving it while the weather lasts. With pitchforks they'll gather what the baler leaves behind. Mrs. Rudd will bring out the flask, the salad. They will lean against the bales and eat their fill. Laughter will carry up the avenue, clear, like birdcall over water.

'It's another fine day.' You feel the need for speech.

Your mother makes some animal sound in her throat. You turn to look at her. She wipes her eyes with the back of her hand. She's never made any allowance for tears.

'Is Eugene up?' she says.

'I don't know. I didn't hear him.'

'I'll go and wake him.'

It's going on for six. Still an hour before you leave. The saucepan boils and you go over to lower the flame. Inside, three eggs knock against each other. One is cracked, a ribbon streaming white. You turn down the gas, watch the eggs. You don't like yours soft.

Eugene comes down wearing his Sunday clothes. He looks tired. He looks much the same as he always does.

'Well, Sis,' he says. 'Are you all set?'

'Yeah.'

'You have your ticket and everything?'

'I do.'

Your mother puts out the cups and plates, slices a quarter out of the loaf. The knife is old, its teeth worn in places. You eat the bread, drink the tea. You taste the soda and wonder what Americans eat for breakfast. Eugene tops his egg, butters bread for the dogs. Nobody says anything. The cuckoo comes out of the clock and calls six times.

'There's a couple of things I've to do up the yard,' Eugene says. 'I won't be long.'

'That's all right.'

'You'd want to leave on time,' your mother says. 'You might get a puncture.'

You place your dirty dishes on the draining board. You have nothing to say to your mother. If you started, you would say the wrong things and you wouldn't want it to end that way. You go upstairs but you'd rather not go back into the room. You stand on the landing. They start talking in the kitchen but you don't hear what they say. A sparrow swoops down on to the window ledge and pecks at his reflection, his beak striking the glass. You watch him until you can't watch him any longer and he flies away.

Your mother didn't want a big family. Sometimes, when she lost her temper, she told you she would put you in a bucket, and drown you. As a child you imagined being taken by force to the edge of the Slaney River, being placed in a bucket, and the bucket being flung out from the bank, floating for a while before it sank; as you grew older you knew it was only a figure of speech, and then you believed it was just an awful thing to say. People sometimes said awful things.

Your eldest sister was sent off to the finest boarding school in Ireland, and became a schoolteacher. Eugene was gifted in school but when he turned fourteen your father pulled him out to work the land. In the photographs the eldest are dressed up: satin ribbons and short trousers, the sun shining in their eyes. The others just came along as nature took its course, were fed and clothed, sent off to the boarding schools. Sometimes they came back for a bank holiday weekend. They brought gifts and an optimism that waned during the days. You could see them remembering everything; the existence, turning rigid when your father's shadow crossed the floor. Leaving, they'd feel cured, impatient to get away.

Your turn never came. By then your father saw no point in educating girls. You'd go off and someone else would have the benefit of your education. If you were sent to day school you could help in the house, the yard. Your father moved into the other room but your mother gave him sex on his birthday. She'd go into his room and they'd have it there. It never took long and they never made noise but you knew. And then that stopped too and you were sent instead, to sleep with your father. It happened once a month or so, and always when Eugene was out.

You went willingly at first: crossed the landing in your nightdress, put your head on his arm. He played with you, praised you, told you you had the brains, that you were the brightest child. Always he put his arm under your neck, then the terrible hand reaching down under the clothes to pull up the nightdress; the fingers, strong from milking, finding you. The mad hand going at himself until he groaned and then him asking you to reach over for the cloth, saying

213

you could go then, if you wanted. The mandatory kiss at the end, stubble and cigarettes on the breath. Sometimes he gave you a cigarette of your own and you could lie beside him smoking, pretending you were someone else. You'd go into the bathroom when it was over and wash, telling yourself it meant nothing, hoping the water would be hot.

Now you stand on the landing trying to remember happiness, a good day, an evening, a kind word. It seems apt to search for something happy to make the parting harder but nothing comes to mind. Instead you remember that time the setter had all those pups. It was around the same time your mother started sending you into his room. You remember standing in the spout-house, your mother leaning over the half barrel, holding the sack down under the water until the whimpering stopped and the sack went still. That day she drowned the pups, she turned her head and looked at you, and smiled.

E ugene comes up and finds you standing there. 'It doesn't matter,' he says. 'Pay no heed.'

'What doesn't matter?'

He shrugs and goes into the room he shares with your father. You drag the suitcase downstairs. Your mother hasn't washed the dishes. She is standing there at the door with a bottle of holy water. She shakes some of the water on you. Some of it gets into your eyes. Eugene comes down with the car keys.

'Da wants to talk to you.'

'He's not getting up?'

'No. You're to go up.'

'Go on,' Ma says. 'Don't leave here empty-handed.'

You go back up the stairs, stop outside his room. You haven't gone through this door since the blood started, since you were twelve. You open it. It's dim inside, stripes of summer light around the curtains. There's that same old smell of cigarette smoke, and feet. You look at his shoes and socks beside the bed. You feel sick. He sits up in his vest, the cattle dealer's eyes taking it all in, measuring.

'So you're going to America,' he says.

You say you are.

'Aren't you the sly one? Will it be warm out there?'

You say it will.

'Will there be anyone to meet you?'

'Yes.' Agree with him. Always, that was your strategy.

'That's all right, so.'

You wait for him to get the wallet out or to tell you where it is, to fetch it. Instead, he puts his hand out. You don't want to touch him but maybe the money is in his hand. In desperation you extend yours, and he shakes it. He draws you towards him. He wants to kiss you. You don't have to look at him to know he's smiling. You pull away, turn out of the room but he calls you back. This is his way. He'll give it to you now that he knows you thought you'd get nothing.

'And another thing,' he says, 'Tell Eugene I want those meadows knocked by dark.'

You go out and close the door. In the bathroom you wash your hands, your face, compose yourself once more.

'I hope he gave you money?' your mother says.

'He did,' you say.

'How much did he give you?'

'A hundred pound.'

'He broke his heart,' she says. 'His own daughter, the last of ye, and he wouldn't even get out of the bed and you going to America. Wasn't it a black bastard I married!'

'Are you ready?' Eugene says. 'We better hit the road.'

You put your arms around your mother. You don't know why. She changes when you do this. You can feel her getting soft in your arms.

'I'll send word, Ma, when I get there.'

'Do,' she says.

'It'll be night before I do.'

'I know,' she says. 'The journey's long.'

Eugene takes the suitcase and you follow him outside. The cherry trees are bending. *The stronger the wind, the stronger the tree.* The sheep dogs follow you. You walk on, past the flowerbeds, the pear trees, on out towards the car. The Cortina is parked under the chestnut's shade. You can smell the wild mint beside the diesel tank. Eugene turns the engine and tries to make some joke, starts down the avenue. You look again at your handbag, your ticket, the passport. You will get there, you tell yourself. They will meet you.

Eugene stops in the avenue before the gates. 'Da gave you nothing, sure he didn't?'

'What?'

'I know he didn't. You needn't let on.'

'It doesn't matter.'

'All I have is a twenty-pound note. I can send you money later on.'

'It doesn't matter.'

'Do you think it would be safe to send money in the post?'

It is a startling question. 'Safe?'

'Yeah.'

You say you think it will.

You get out and open the gates. He drives through, stops to wait for you. As you put the wire on, the filly trots down to the edge of the field, leans up against the fence, and whinnies. She's a red chestnut with one white stocking. You sold her to buy your ticket but she will not be collected until tomorrow. That was the arrangement. You watch her and turn away but it's impossible not to look back. Your eyes follow the gravel road, the strip of green between the tracks, on up to the granite post left there from Protestant days and, past it, your mother who has come out to see the last of you. She waves a cowardly little wave, and you wonder if she will ever forgive you for leaving her there with her husband.

On down the avenue, the Rudds are already in the meadows. There's a shot from an engine as something starts, a bright clap of laughter. You pass Barna Cross where you used to catch the bus to the Community School. Towards the end, you hardly bothered going. You simply sat in the wood under the trees all day or, if it was raining, you found a hayshed. Sometimes you read the books your sisters left behind. Sometimes you fell asleep. Once a man came into his hayshed and found you there. You kept your eyes closed. He stood there for a long time and then he went away.

'There's something you should know,' Eugene says.

'Oh?'

'I'm not staying.'

'What do you mean?'

'I'm giving up the land. They can keep it.'

'What?'

'Can you see me living there with them until the end of their days? Could you see me bringing a woman in? What woman could stand it? I'd have no life.'

'But what about all the work you've done, all that time?'

'I don't care about any of that,' he says. 'All that is over.'

'Where will you go?'

'I don't know. I'll rent some place.'

'Where?'

'I don't know yet. I was waiting until you left. I didn't think any further.'

'You didn't stay on my account?'

He slows the car and looks over. 'I did,' he says. 'But I wasn't much use was I, Sis?'

It is the first time anyone has ever mentioned it. It feels like a terrible thing, being said.

'You couldn't be there all the time.'

'No,' he says. 'I suppose I couldn't.'

Between Baltinglass and Blessington the road winds. You remember this part of the road. You came this way for the All-Ireland finals. Your father had a sister in Tallaght he could stay with, a hard woman who made great tarts and left a chain of smoke. Boggy fields, bad land, surround this road, and a few ponies grazing. As a child, you thought this was The West of Ireland. It used to make the adults laugh, to hear you say it. And now you suddenly remember one good thing about your father. It was before you had begun to go into his room. He had gone into the village and stopped at the garage for petrol. The girl at the pumps came up to him and told him she was the brightest girl in the class, the best at every subject until you came along. He'd come back from the village and repeated this, and he was proud because you were brighter than the Protestant's daughter.

Close to the airport, planes appear in the sky. Eugene parks the car and helps you find the desk. Neither one of you knows exactly what to do. They look at your passport, take your suitcase and tell you where to go. You step on to moving stairs that frighten you. There's a coffee shop where Eugene tries to make you eat a fry but you don't want to eat or stay and keep him company.

Your brother embraces you. You have never been embraced this way. When his stubble grazes your face, you pull back.

'I'm sorry,' he says.

'It's all right.'

'Goodbye, Sis.'

'Goodbye, Eugene. Take care.'

'Watch out for pickpockets in New York.'

You cannot answer.

'Write,' he says quickly. 'Don't forget to write.'

'I won't. Don't worry.'

You follow passengers through a queue and leave him behind. He will not go back for the fry; he hasn't the time. You did not have to deliver the message. You know he will put his boot down, be home before noon, have those meadows knocked before dark. After that there will be corn to cut. Already the winter barley's turning. September will bring more work, old duties to the land: sheds to clean out, cattle to test, lime to spread, dung. You know he will never leave the fields.

A stranger asks for your handbag, and you give it to him. You pass through a frame that has no door and your handbag is returned to you. On the other side, the lights are bright. There's the smell of perfume and roasted coffee beans: expensive things. You make out bottles of tanning lotion, a rack of dark glasses. It is all getting hazy but you keep on going, because you must, past the T-shirts and the duty free towards the gate. When you find it, there is hardly anyone there but you know this is the place. You look for another door, make out part of a woman's body. You push it and it opens. You pass bright hand-basins, mirrors. Someone asks are you all right—such a stupid question—but you do not cry until you have opened and closed another door, until you have safely locked yourself inside your stall.

☐

RESOLUTION

The First South Central Australian Expedition

Jim Shepard

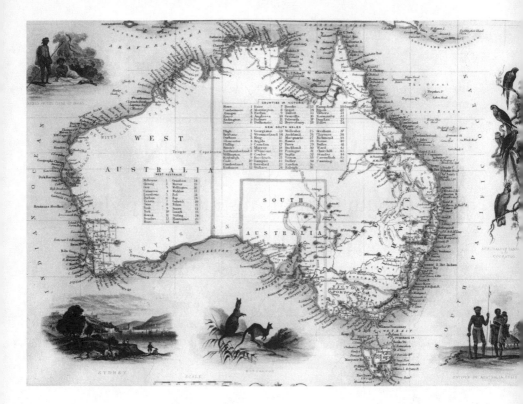

April 1st, 1840

The three of us traded Christmas tales during our long portage. Hill and Browne both professed shock at my contribution, which seemed less than shocking to me. I had related to them the method by which my father, with what I remember to be the sad-eyed support of our mother, celebrated Our Lord's birth each Christmas Day.

Having had three sons, myself the eldest, he had resolved, he said, to no longer be tyrannized by the understanding that during this particular Season he was obligated as a Christian to provide even more provision for his family, by way of gifts, than he did in the course of the normal round. Henceforth, then, one and only one child each year would be favoured with a lovely gift to commemorate the Day. He hoped that the others would derive the pleasure they should from their brother's good fortune. In accordance with his understanding of the general workings of the natural world, the process would proceed by lot, and not cyclically. So it was entirely possible that one child would be favoured by chance, two or even three years in a row. We would all find out only upon coming downstairs on Christmas morning, to see what was set about the hearth.

He made this announcement having gathered the family together on Christmas Eve the year I turned five. My brothers, being at the time only three and two, hardly knew what they were being told. His wife and our mother, by all accounts gay and outgoing before her marriage, stood by while he entertained questions about his decision, and then did her best to salvage some measure of wan cheer over the course of those Christmas Days that followed.

My story was greeted with an extended silence. We were having some trouble with the horses in the current. Browne announced himself, finally, to have been cudgelled about the head by the damned thing. He meant my story. Hill found it odd that such a father would have shown a willingness to finance a part of the expedition. 'I'm sure it's not entirely unusual,' I remarked to them, sometime later, about my father's notion of gift-giving.

'I'm sure it is,' Browne responded.

April 3rd

My father instilled in me the habit of resolving every day to make a resolution, to be repeated aloud when dressing and undressing. Today's has been: 'Think well before giving an answer, and never speak except from strong convictions.' 'Are you conversing with yourself?' Browne asked from outside my tent, this morning, when he overheard.

The rock here is of an oolitic limestone, and treacherous with hollows throughout. The surrounding area is beset by stupendous tufts of porcupine grass (spinifex), four to five feet high. The country so far has been stupefyingly consistent. We are now fifteen weeks out and for the last six have continued to wait for some kind of happy transformation in the path ahead.

We stopped at a marshy creek and it came on raining, and Cuppage shot himself. Somehow, in stowing his saddle, a loop caught the trigger. The ball came out his back under the shoulder.

Our legs are full of the sharp ends of the spinifex. Large numbers of crows are following the baggage train, apparently for the sheep's offals.

April 5th

We have left a note as to our progress in a bottle in the fork of the great gum tree at Sadness Creek, per our arrangement, to be carried back to Adelaide by a Native sent for that purpose. The bottle is marked in an indelible ink 'South Central Australian Expedition, R. M. Beadle'.

The animals have been watered and are resting under fair and mild skies. We have been so anxious to proceed at all speed that I have not set down in these pages the full catalogue of our expedition. In the matter of personnel, I can state without equivocation that I was given a free hand, and chose a crew of twelve out of the over three hundred able-bodied men who applied for positions. Any group of men isolated on a long journey is entirely dependent upon one another, and we will be no exception. Accompanying me on this undertaking are:

Officers.
James A. Browne. Second in command
Richard Scott Hill. Expedition physician.
Philip Mander-Jones. Expedition draughtsman and surveyor.

Men.
Edgar Birks. In charge of stock.
D. K. Hamilton & Charles Mabberly. To man the whaleboat.
John Gould. In charge of the horses.
Robert Cuppage. Armourer.
Francis Purdie. Cook.
John Mack & H. L. Moorhouse. Bullock drivers.

We carry five tons of provisions and equipment on three bullock drays, and two horse carriages pulled by draught horses. One of the carriages transports the whaleboat. Each of the loaded drays weighs over two thousand pounds. We began with a ton of flour alone, three hundred pounds of bacon, and a quarter-ton of sugar. We carry for safety a pairing of sextants, artificial horizons, prismatic compasses and barometers. A ream of foolscap, this book for journal-keeping, sealing wax, camel's hair brushes, an inkstand, ink, goose quills, coloured pencils and a sketch-palette. Five revolvers and two rifles. For ornithological specimens, a shotgun. As well as all the necessary ammunition. And a trunk of trade and gift items, primarily hats and knives, for the Aborigines. In the back of the train are four extra horses, one hundred head of sheep for provision and four dogs for herding the sheep. Our procession extends back over a quarter of a mile.

We have been empowered to strike north from Mt Arden into the great interior as far as the twenty-eighth parallel of latitude. This in order to determine whether a mountain range or other major height of land exists in that vicinity. Governor Gawler and Lord Russell have to that end approved a budget of two thousand five hundred pounds, for an undertaking not to exceed twelve months.

If such a height of land does exist, then everything north of it must necessarily flow into an as-yet undiscovered watershed: a vast inland sea.

April 7th
Today's resolution: 'Strive, and hold cheap the strain.' We have set a guard, and impressed the men with the necessity of vigilance. And with the danger of the journey ahead. Tomorrow we step off into the first truly daunting territory, leaving the southern watershed behind. The Aborigines call our resting-place Dead Man's Flat. The men in high

spirits, the animals in good order. Up late, too agitated for sleep, my mind full of a thousand small tasks, and marvelling on this strange, strange country, where even the celestial sphere is the wrong way about.

April 8th
Even as a child, I'd pressed my hand to the map of Australia in my *Boys' Atlas*, palming the blank upon its centre. Our biggest cities are but specks perched on the extreme southern and eastern tips of a vast unknown. Men of perseverance and resource have failed to penetrate that remote and oblique vastness. The entire area seems so fearsomely defended by deserts, one might suppose Nature has intentionally closed it to civilized man.

Browne has pointed out to me in the privacy of my tent that Lord Russell and Governor Gawler's charge says nothing about an inland sea. My father, too, tried to strike the boat from the budget-list. Browne believes, with them, that the great centre is likely to prove in its entirety to be inhospitable desert. But I paid the cost of the whaleboat with my own funds. Explorers have recorded countless westward-flowing streams, none of which empty into the Southern Ocean. Where do these waters go if not to an immense sea or lake to which there must exist a navigable entrance? I believe the continent to be fashioned like a bowl, with elevated sides and a sunken centre. A bowl whose lowest points are likely to be filled with water. 'A bowl,' Browne said, with some unhappiness, when I outlined for him my thinking.

And imagine if that sea disembogues into the northern ocean, by way of some strait, I reminded him. 'The Beadle Sea,' he smiled, as though indulging a child he loved very much. We were together relashing the bundle containing our charter and various maps, such as they were. 'The Browne Strait,' I added, in order to see him smile again.

April 10th
Browne, too, has had a vexed relationship with his father. His father's unfortunate speculations in corn when Browne was still a child left the family nearly without resource. He admitted during his interview that he had reaped few benefits, emotional or financial, from his parents. He has, nevertheless, turned himself into a young man of no little account. He brings to our group an artist's spirit and a Zouave's resourcefulness. As well as an apostate's scepticism. During a supper

'A COVER-TO-COVER BARGAIN.'

TIME OUT

'ESSENTIAL READING.' OBSERVER

POST: Granta Magazine, PO Box 6712, Brunel Road, Basingstoke, RG24 4F
TEL/FAX: In the UK: FreeCall 0500 004 033. Outside UK: tel 44 (0)1256 302 8
fax 44 (0)1256 812 358 • subs@granta.com

YES!

I'D LIKE TO SUBSCRIBE FOR MYSELF FOR:

- ◯ 1 year (4 issues) at just £27.95 **30% OFF**
- ◯ 2 years (8 issues) at just £51.95 **35% OFF**
- ◯ 3 years (12 issues) at just £71.95 **40% OFF**

PLEASE START MY SUBSCRIPTION WITH ◯ this issue ◯ next issue

I'D LIKE TO GIVE A GIFT SUBSCRIPTION FOR:

- ◯ 1 year (4 issues) at just £27.95
- ◯ 2 years (8 issues) at just £51.95
- ◯ 3 years (12 issues) at just £71.95

PLEASE START THE SUBSCRIPTION WITH ◯ this issue ◯ next issue

MY DETAILS (please supply even if ordering a gift): Mr/Ms/Mrs/Miss:

_____

City/Postcode/Country

6HBG95

GIFT RECIPIENT'S DETAILS (if applicable): Mr/Ms/Mrs/Miss:

_____

City/Postcode/Country

TOTAL* £_____ by ◯ £ cheque enclosed (to 'Granta') ◯ Visa/MCard/AmEx:

card no __ __ __ __ __ __ __ __ __ __ __ __ __ __ __ __

expiry date __ __ / __ __ signature _____

* <u>POSTAGE</u>. The prices stated include UK postage. For the rest of Europe, please add £8 (per year). For the rest of the world, please add £15 (per year).

<u>DATA PROTECTION</u>. Please tick here if you do not want to receive occasional offers and mailings from compatible organizations. ◯

gathering of the officers I listed the altogether beneficial ways in which our various virtues interacted. Hill, I pointed out, besides his skills as a healer, is also a man of refined manners, a genteel disposition and a sensitive temperament. Mander-Jones has a scientist's exactitude and love of order. Our virtues together, I suggested, comprised one ideal explorer. 'Of frustrated ambitions,' Browne pointed out. A short while after our discussion, one of the men shot what Mander-Jones informs us is a new sort of butcherbird, very scarce and wild.

April 13th
Today's resolution: 'To love is to be all made of sighs and tears; to be all made of faith and service.' Named a dry creek bed of some size Birks Creek, to reward the fellow for the labour of having surveyed it. Sufficient saltbush, which the horses eat readily. Some small, fawn-coloured kangaroo, of which the dogs have killed four.

No elevation of any kind breaks the horizon or varies the sea of scrub ahead. At first there will be the appearance of improvement, then barren country again. During our evening meal Browne asked if the Governor or Lord Russell had any knowledge of the whaleboat. I told him that they had made clear to my satisfaction that they had every confidence in myself and my decisions. Cuppage reports that his pain is very bad when he mounts or dismounts. Browne considers it a poor sign that our armourer has managed to shoot himself.

April 14th
All day the sun through heavy clouds, which checked some of its fiery beams. Nothing about but a few coleopterous insects. 'Beetles,' Browne corrects me, a little peevishly. After encampment we observed four or five signal fires. The Aborigines are apparently retreating before our advance.

April 16th
No sign of a previous civilization. Not an arrowhead, not a flint, not even the remains of a cooking-fire. Everything suggests an ongoing and immemorial enervation. A kind of trance in the air.

April 20th
A stretch of better country, over which we have made good progress.

Found a native wheat, a beautiful oat and a rye; and in hollows a blue or purple vetch of which the cattle are very fond. In one stretch, an entire plain covered with perfectly spherical stones. Formed by the action of water, no doubt, when the plain was—or is—undersea.

At times the land ahead is as flat as a table. The birds are remarkable: ibis with their coral eyes; emus, striding about like enormous indignant chickens on their startling claws. Olive-green and yellow butcherbirds circling on their updraughts to gain height. Something Mander-Jones calls a 'ventriloquist dove', which, with no movement of its throat, makes a sound that seems to come from the distant horizon. We are taking notes and collecting specimens whenever possible. We all feel the exhilaration of putting our other lives behind us. Mack, with Cuppage laid up, has had unusual success shooting pigeons. Today's resolution: 'Look round the habitable world! How few know their own good; or knowing it, pursue.'

April 21st

A close, humid day which produced an incessant clamminess over the body, and called forth innumerable insects. Mander-Jones bitten on the scalp by centipede in his hat. The dogs killed a fine specimen of something that had been following us, but in the ensuing scuffle they tore off its head. It rained gently in the morning.

April 22nd

When I was less than five years old, I am told, I dragged around behind me on a cord a legless horse to which I was inseparably attached. The poor thing bounced and tumbled along in a most pitiful way, as I remember. No one knew whence it came. It was a carved lump of pine painted with a blue saddle. It had a mouth but no eyes. I slept with it and named it My Captain, for reasons which also puzzled those who gave it any thought.

April 23rd

Plagued by the flies, and in the draws and rocky places, the death adders and other snakes. Eight-inch centipedes with ghastly jaws, fearless, mouse-sized scorpions and ubiquitous stinging ants. Men glad of moving on.

Browne at our officers' supper again lodged a complaint

concerning the number of water casks we carry (two), which he sees as woefully inadequate. He reminded us all that we're doing what we've been expressly advised by those familiar with the country not to do: travel with no line of communication to our rear and no maps for our forward journey. His reassuring prudence was duly recorded. In order to demonstrate our congruency on this point I cited for him yesterday's resolution, which was, 'Take care of the minutes, for the hours will take care of themselves.'

During heavy winds the dogs shelter in low gullies, whining and barking to very little purpose.

April 24th
Finally, some natives. A small group: two men, four women and a few children. They were camped on some sand hills and watched as we approached. The children, though, were in a terrible fright, and clung to their mothers like opossum. The adults are very wiry and strong-looking though they tend to be deficient in the front tooth. While we watched they cooked some mice in the hot sand itself and then devoured them entire, fur, entrails and all, nipping off the tail with their teeth. I had with me a vocabulary of the *Language of the Murray Natives*, but was unable to make them understand a word of it. We asked, by signs, where they derived their water, and they intimated that they depended on rain. They did so by lifting their hands and then pulling them quickly down while fluttering their fingers. Then they pointed where we were headed and shook their heads vigorously.

They were much taken with our appearance, and some of us do present a sight: Mabberly with his great buccaneer's hat, Birks with his peculiar facial scar, Mander-Jones with his filthy beard. And Hill's spectacles, which are so very small that I constantly wonder how he sees adequately through them. Purdie, the only one of our party to have met Aborigines on their home ground before, informed us after we had moved on that they believe Europeans to be blackfellows returned from the grave, turned white because of their new status as ghosts.

Tested the water in their water hole and found it to be 107.8 degrees. Tonight the dogs are barking towards the point from which the wind is coming. One of the horses kicked Moorhouse's gun on the stock and shivered it to pieces. Hill has broken my watch.

Jim Shepard

April 27th
Dreadful passage. For three days now our road lay over these abominable and rotten lands on which water has evidently subsided and whose surface the sun has cracked into deep fissures. Whenever the dray wheels drop into the holes it shocks the animals greatly. We are flanked as we proceed by great ridges of basalt and ironstone. Nothing seems tempered by weathering; all edges seem razor-sharp. There is much eurite, as well, underfoot. Mysterious columnar formations off to the west. Nearly all we survey seems unavailable to cultivation. The temperature yesterday rose to 111 Fahrenheit; this morning it fell to 38. Nights we huddle in flannel pantaloons and greatcoats. Days we suffer in the heat. How it is possible that the Natives can withstand such extremes, unprovided as they are against the heat and cold?

Cuppage is now able to lift or carry very little. Hill fears his wound may be infected.

May 1st
Full of accidents today. Moorhouse's dray broke its axle-pole, and Gould's its rear wheel. The country is more open and worse in character. Rents and fissures so tremendous the cart-drivers are thrown from their seats. Mabberly has been admirably careful with the whaleboat, about which, considering the likelihood of her being soon wanted, I am naturally nervous. Nothing cheering in the prospect to the N and NW. One of the dogs has been lost— swallowed—in a strange dry salt lagoon comprised of gypsum and black mud. Its compatriots were hysterical with grief and upset. The approaches to the place were most unpleasantly spongy and soft. The wind blows salt from it over the flats behind us like smoke. Old Fitz, our best draught horse, has a swelling on his near hind leg.

May 2nd
Stopped to give the animals a day of rest and repair the drays. At a dry creek bed, some white mallow, which Gould gave to the horses. Nearer the creek a plant with a striped and bitter fruit. Perhaps some kind of cucumber.

The flies an affliction. Scaled a box tree to consider the path ahead with the telescope. Flies blocked and clogged the eyepiece. Attacked by ants, their bites like a bad sunburn, throughout the night.

May 5th
I've directed that the bullocks be fastened by the noses to the carts, so that we might start earlier. The thermometer this morning at half past six stood at 102. Increasingly the only plants we encounter are differing kinds of atriplex with their terrible spines. The only water our advance parties were able to discover today was a puddle so thick with animalculae as to be unfit to drink.

Numerous insects about at night. During the day, the flies. Whether we are out taking bearings or in gullies searching for water or in our tents, it is all the same. They watch our movements and, the moment our hands are full, settle in swarms on our faces.

May 12th
A new mortification: we have left behind all scrub and rock to confront gigantic sandy ridges which succeed each other like wave trains, and we climb and descend one just to confront another. Only the smallest, umbrella-shaped shrubs in evidence here and there, the surface heat having seared away the lower branches. The ridges are sixty to seventy feet high and as steep as ocean swells in a heavy gale. They appear to extend many miles to the NW. Should we find a body of water in that direction, I am at a loss as to how we would negotiate the dray with the whaleboat that distance.

Even so, the ridges exhibit a regularity that waves alone must have created. What we are struggling with, it follows, was not long ago a sub-marine position. 'Oh, for the love of God,' Browne responded, his hat soaked through with sweat even before our day had begun, when I told him.

May 19th
A week of stupefying labour. The heavily loaded drays sink deep into the sand and the overheated bullocks just cease their struggles completely for minutes at a time. The days are scorching hot and the animals are suffering greatly. Today the sheep came to a dead halt and would not move, while the dogs and horses huddled under and against the drays for such shade as they might provide, and remained there until evening.

Winds and whirlwinds, all oven-hot. Our legs and our horses' legs are pierced in a hundred places by spinifex, which has in the last two days begun to cover the ridges. The horses are suffering even more than we might have expected. Both Captain and the chestnut have had a running at the nose which I feared to be glanders, but Gould reports they are better. I have an ugly rash over my back and chest. The men complain of insomnia and sore eyes. This evening at sunset we remarked upon an extended haze on the horizon opposite the sun, of a supernatural blue. The effect, we presume, of refraction.

I have had some surprisingly bitter contentions with some of the other officers. More than ever I am persuaded that the interior is only to be achieved by careful calculation and that more headlong rushing about will only lead us into difficulty. As it is now, advance parties, usually captained by Browne, scout twenty to thirty miles ahead of us by horse. Both Browne and Mander-Jones believe we cannot maintain this unhurried pace with summer only four or five months away.

I hope I will not shrink from the trials ahead. The day may come when I must face greater extremes, and I trust I will do so not the less firmly for having only the smallest notion of what I'm likely to encounter.

May 22nd
Cuppage feverish and laid-up. A comfortable pallet has been arranged for him in the whaleboat. A few days' inactivity while the advance parties search for water. I have directed that the whaleboat be outfitted and painted.

Hill has been working wonders with poor Cuppage's suffering. Hill is really like a young hero from literature: fair-minded, virile, eager to get on. He articled as a surgeon, which he found not very agreeable. His real passion is for astronomy. He has a sense of direction so intuitive he negotiated alone some of the jungles on the northern coast. And few men have less of envy in their disposition.

All of Adelaide, it seemed, approved my choice of Hill for this expedition. And nearly as many lamented my choice of Browne. This man with the instincts and fearlessness of a Native in the bush, and of a judgement beyond his station, is in Adelaide a drunkard of the lowest reputation. Hill initially and privately expressed surprise that I would suffer such a man to be in my party, and my father, too, expressed violent doubts. But here in the wild there is not a more ingenious and valuable follower to be found. I believe him to be personally attached to me, and nurse the fervent belief that this chance at achievement will have a decisive effect on the rest of his life.

May 28th

Our progress renewed. Today's resolution: 'Seek experience joined to common sense, which to mortals is a providence.' The ascents are backbreaking and the revelations at the summits unrewarding.

Still little seasonal cooling. The sun dries everything with such speed that one can almost watch the few pools we do find sink. There is no way of knowing how soon we might be cut off by the loss of water holes behind us. The complete absence of animal life is stark evidence of the dire poverty of what lies all around us, and ahead. We are now alone in the wilderness. The wind is blowing from the NE in our faces with the heat of a blacksmith's forge. Despite our exertions, none of us exhibit any moisture on the skin. This is perhaps related to our being now much distressed by violent headaches.

May 29th

Continued all day without knowing whether we were extricating or ensnaring ourselves. We are to all intents and purposes at sea. A carrion kite hovered over us early this morning in befuddlement at our presence.

June 2nd

Recovering in our tents. Supper of a little dried beef. Browne reminded us that we are in a precarious situation, and that the least mistake will be lethal. This is a region in which we have not the leisure to pause. He further pointed out that it wasn't the advance but the retreat that was to be most dreaded.

June 3rd

No travel. Old Fitz now dead lame. The men employed examining the bacon. Today's resolution: 'Of comfort, no man speak.' Surface heat so great we can't hold stones we pick up with our hand.

June 4th
No travel.

June 5th
Another halt. The men complain of giddiness when they stoop. The bullocks done in. The heat of the sand is so intense that the poor animals paw away the top layers to get to the cooler beneath. The upper leathers of Hill's shoes are burnt away. Gould's back terribly blistered. The dogs are losing the pads of their feet. The Natives could not possibly walk this desert at midsummer. The bullocks' yokes are even now so heated the men cannot handle them. We ride with our feet out of the stirrups, because the irons are too hot. Mander-Jones's chronometer has stopped. It is no longer possible to use the quills, the ink dries so rapidly. 119 degrees in the sun.

The monotony of such plodding, hour after hour, always with the prospect of waking the next morning to more of the same—! We are nearly silent during this apathy of motion. This coma of riding. Even a small object becomes an achievement when attained, something on which to focus the mind in so demoralizing a vista.

June 9th
I could not more regret the paucity of casks to hold water. I would strongly recommend casks as indispensable on all future expeditions in this country. There is a yellow hue on the horizon each morning, which we now understand to be a sure indication of the afternoon's insupportable heat.

June 12th
We have come upon what can only be called the Stony Desert, the first sight of which caused us to lose our breath. It is more demoralizing than what has gone before. Not a speck of plant life across the horizon. Masses of rock mixed with white quartz split into innumerable fragments. Ruin and desolation, stretching out in an endless plain as far as we can see. Purdie whimpered audibly from his seat on one of the drays at the prospect. Some of the men laughed.

The surfaces are diamond-hard and ring under our horses' shoes. The stone is so thick upon the ground that the carts leave no track. Distance travelled fourteen miles.

June 14th

It is as if the earth itself were steel-shod. The horses' hooves are being cut to the quick. We're shaken by detonations to our right and left: great rock masses splitting off in the extremes of temperature. Seven sheep dead from the heat. Distance travelled eleven miles.

Today a new stretch of rock hued with iron oxide, so that the plains ahead now have a dark purple cast. The country continues to raise terrible havoc with the horses' shoes, which are wearing away like wax. Gould and Mack report that their headaches have worsened. The men complain of rheumatism and most of us have violent pains in our hip joints. Hill reports a large ring round the moon last night, most likely indicative of wind. The whaleboat suffered today its first accident: its stern sheets were torn off on a rock. It was not the driver's fault, but mine, for not warning him of its proximity. Each day brings fresh sheaves of anxiety to add to our already overstuffed bundle.

June 15th

We are all on foot to spare the horses. The stone is in no way rounded, and brutal to the feet. Gould complains incessantly of an excruciating pain in his forehead. Poor Cuppage has not been heard from for days, and only cries out when the whaleboat is shaken by a drop or a crash. Browne's horse has an inflammation of the mucous membrane. The casks are empty. At the first waterless halt, the horses would not eat, and collected round me, my poor Captain much afflicted and tugging my hat with his teeth to claim attention. I asked Moorhouse to reconnoitre the extent of the ridges to our NW from the vantage point of the ridge to our W. His climb provided him, regrettably, with no cover. He returned to pronounce it the most difficult task he had ever performed.

June 20th

Only three miles down a ravine to our E, a kind of natural oasis, with a pool thirty to forty feet wide and nearly ten feet deep situated beneath the shade of large stands of casuarina and mulga trees. Ample feed for the animals. Providence has guided us to the only place in this desert where our wants might be supplied for any amount of time, but has also here stayed our progress in a region soon to become forbidden ground.

Today completes the sixth month of our absence from Adelaide. How much longer we shall be out it is impossible to say. We still wait for winter rains. I am heartbroken at the delay. I remain of the full conviction that we're fifty miles or less from the Inland Sea. My only consolation is that the present situation is unavoidable.

June 27th

I have been neglecting my resolutions. Today's is: 'The happy man finds in some part of his soul a drop of patience.' I have been trying to chart our position and finding it impossible to put pencil to paper in this super-heated tent. Have set the men to digging a chamber deep in the ground from which we might make our calculations.

June 30th

Birks has a pulmonary condition. Was bled yesterday and is better today. Mabberly has had an attack of inflammation of the lungs. Almost everyone is complaining of bleeding at the nose. We are all beset by symptoms of scurvy. My gums are so sore that I cannot take even porridge and have a vile taste of copper in my mouth, with savage headaches. We all trust the symptoms will not increase, because soon we must move at all risks and under any circumstances. Our diet is unwholesome. We must collect something in the way of a vegetable.

Cuppage is now insensible. We have discussed whether to send him back and Hill has ventured that he would never survive the journey. Neither would whoever accompanied him, Browne has added grimly. He returned, his horse lathered and nearly broken, to report that the water holes to our rear, at which we not six days ago found ample water, have now no moisture left in their beds. Our retreat is cut off. We are bound here as fast as though we were on an ice floe in the great Arctic ocean.

July 1st

The barometer remains unyielding. Until it falls we have no hope of rain. I have reduced the allowance of tea and sugar. The men have become as improvident as Aborigines. The inactivity is causing between us much vexation and anxiety. About thirty sheep remaining. Have set the men to repacking and inspecting the bacon and biscuit. The bran in which the bacon was packed is now entirely saturated and heavier than the meat. Our wax candles have melted. Our hair has stopped growing.

July 6th

I was born here in Australia, though this is not commonly known. The year of my tenth birthday, my brothers and I were sent to England with my mother's elder sister. We would not see our parents again for more than a decade. We lived variously with relatives, always in close proximity to lives of enormous privilege. I was offered various playmates, each of whom I detested. Where were my friends? Where was that person for whom my happiness was an outcome to be desired? I led my brothers on a midnight ramble in search of home. They were eight and seven, and complained about neither the distance nor the cold. The younger, Humphrey, was shoeless. I was so moved by their fortitude that I was teary-eyed through the march. We begged milk from a farmer and were rounded up by a constable the following afternoon.

Browne too hated school. He remembered with fierce indignation a headmaster's remark that God had created boys' buttocks in order to facilitate the learning of Latin.

July 12th

I am much concerned about Browne. His behaviour has alarmed both Mander-Jones and Hill. He has been refusing water and crouching for stretches out of the shade, hatless. I have tried to provide him with duties that will keep his faculties engaged. A flight of swifts passed over high to the NW at twilight. They were beating against the wind.

July 24th

The same sun, morning to night. We might save ourselves the trouble of taking measurements. The ants at sundown swarm under our coverings. The flies intensify at dawn. All manner of crawling and flying insects fill our clothes. There never was a country such as this for stabbing, biting or stinging things.

Our scurvy is worse. It must be dreadful in its advanced stages, for even as it is we are nearly undone. 'I have today's resolution,' Browne said to me this morning, lying on the floor of our dugout room. He hadn't spoken for a day. His head rested on Hill's feet. 'Always remember that Love is the wisdom of the fool and the folly of the wise,' he said.

What on earth were we on about now? Mander-Jones cried out from beside me, in response. I hushed him. 'I am travelling with lunatics,' he said, with great feeling, before lapsing once more into silence.

The men have tipped the whaleboat over to make a shaded lean-to. Today I was the only one willing to leave either shelter to take a reading. The barometer has fallen to a point that would normally suggest rain, but it is impossible to guess what to anticipate here. The water in our oasis is evaporating visibly. It stands now of a depth of only four feet.

August 20th
The eighth month. Midwinter. 112 in the shade, 129 in the sun. The heat has split the unprotected edges of our horses' hooves into fine laminae. Our fingernails are now as brittle as rice paper. The lead falls out of our pencils. Mack and Gould engaged in a fistfight that was quelled only after Gould threatened to stave in his head. In our dugout last night, Browne again could not be moved to speak. Hill's voice was a brave croak. Mander-Jones was sullen and uncommunicative, afflicted as he is with sore eyes from the flies getting into them. I told them that it could only have been that our expedition coincided with the most unfortunate season of drought. Even here it could not be that there were only two recorded days of rain in eight months.

Gould reported that grass was now so deficient about the camp that we could no longer tether the horses.

The success or failure of any undertaking is determined by its leader, I reminded them. Browne roused himself in response. He seemed enraged in ways he wasn't fully able to articulate. He theorized that my choice of bringing extra paint for the boat, rather than adequate casks for water, or lemon or lime juice for scurvy, spoke volumes about the nature of our undertaking. And what was the nature of our undertaking, sir? I asked him. Idiotic, sir, he answered. Criminal, sir. Laughable.

August 22nd

Out of sorts and unable to function, from upset. Hill, after a discreet hesitation of a few hours, took over the direction of the men in terms of their responsibilities. At sundown the entire horizon to the west was indigo with clouds and heavy rain. Each of us spent the evening absorbed in that direction, unwilling to speak.

I dreamed of my father as I saw him on the pier in Adelaide upon my return. When I awoke, Browne was kicking the leg of my cot with his heavy boot. He had today's resolution, he announced. He said, 'There was an old man in a Marsh, Whose manners were futile and harsh.' 'That's not a resolution,' I called after him, once I'd found my voice, once he'd left.

With what energy we've been able to retrieve we have been busy all day preparing an excursion to the WNW to try to meet and retrieve some of that rain. This will decide the fate of our Expedition. We will take six weeks' provisions, one of the casks, and four or five bullock-hides to carry the water back. Browne and I will lead, and Birks, Gould and Mack will accompany us. We'll take seven of the horses and one of the drays.

September 12th

Three weeks out. Set out on August 23rd at four a.m. The cask is now nearly empty. Today we gave our horses as much water as reason would justify before making camp. Their docility under such suffering is heart-rending. They cannot rest and spend the night troublesomely persevering, plodding round the cart, trying to poke their noses into the bung hole. We close our eyes and pretend not to see.

September 16th

A water hole. A triumph for Browne. The water cloudy and off but purer than any we have for some time seen. Filled the cask and made some tea. The horizon again shot through with lightning.

September 21st

Returned to the strictest rationing now that our strength seems somewhat restored. Walking as much as possible to spare the horses. My heels and back lanced with pain. When lying down I feel as if I'm being rolled across a threshing machine. Summer starting to come on. The thermometer between 120 and 133 during the day. Matches held in the hand flare into flame. We must be a sight, I remarked to Browne: burned by the sun, our clothes in rags, our hats long since shapeless with sweat, covered in insects, each absorbed in his private cell of misery, whether a chafing shoe or an open sore. And almost no quarrels. On this never-ending ribbon of interminable heat. Browne, as if to prove my point, did not answer.

September 30th
This morning we gave Captain, my mount, double breakfast, hoping it would strengthen him, but it did not. The poor brute staggered rather than walked along. At midnight he fell. We got him up again and, abandoning his saddle, proceeded. At a mile, though, he fell again, and could not go on. I sat by him in the night as he expired. After he did I was desolate, and took myself off into the darkness for a while. I had fully intended to purchase him at the sale of the remnants of the Expedition, perhaps as a gift for Browne.

October 10th
We have found only a runnel with mud so thick I could not swallow it. Browne managed to drink some of it made into tea. It fell over the lip of his cup like clotted cream, and smeared the horses' noses like clay. They refused it. Browne was then ill all the next day.

October 12th
Some kind of cyclopean stones now before us. Even the horses regard them with dismay. I dismounted and ascended the first for a bearing. It was no trifling task in our condition and in these temperatures. Birks accompanied me with the instruments. 'This is more than a Government day's work, sir,' he said on the way back down.

I could not respond. Our view had been over as terrible a region as Man ever saw. Its aspect was so mortifying that it left us with not a tinge of hope. We have to return, with every promise of a better country before us within reach annihilated. We all stood dumbly in the heat at this understanding, as if concussed by a blow, before eventually returning to our midday shelter under the dray. Mack and Gould wept. Browne kept up an intermittent continuous hum, like a bush insect. Was it possible to give up, having achieved nothing? I asked myself aloud. One of the horses toppled to its knees as if by way of answer. No one spoke again until sundown, when we turned about and headed back the way we came. We have been defeated, I reminded our little group, by obstacles not to be overcome by human perseverance.

Our bearings record that the farthest point to which we penetrated was to Longitude 138.5.00 and Latitude 24.30.00, and I will in truth affirm that no men ever wandered in a more despairing and hopeless desert. I have no other observations to add on the nature of this country.

November 17th

Made camp yesterday at six a.m., nearly done in from lack of food and water. Three of the seven horses lost, and the other four have been made nearly useless. All of us are afflicted by a fatigue that now seems impossible to overcome. The buttons on our shirts are by mid-morning so heated as to pain us. Few men have ever laid themselves down to rest, if it can be called rest, as bereft as I have been today.

November 20th

Browne has somehow managed another expedition to the south on one of the fresher horses to ascertain how much water remains on our line of retreat. He returned this morning to report that one of the deepest and narrowest channels had long gone dry. With that, there can be no water nearer to us than seventy-eight miles, and perhaps not there.

The horses are at their wits' end. What grass there is flies to powder under their tread. The last ram has taken the staggers and Birks has ordered him killed.

Whirlwinds blowing hot all morning from the NE, increased to a heavy gale. The incinerating heat was so withering that I wondered if the very trees would ignite. Everything gave way before it; the horses stood with their backs to the wind and their noses to the ground, without the strength to raise their heads. One of our thermometers, graduated to 157 degrees, burst. Which is a circumstance I believe no traveller on this earth has ever before had to record.

November 24th

A party rebellious to my purposes has put it to me that they intend to strike out to the south in hope of relief. Browne reported this to me. And of whom was this party constituted? I croaked, gazing at him with what I hoped to be severity. Birks, he said. Hamilton and Mabberly. Gould. Cuppage. Purdie. Mack and Moorhouse. And Mander-Jones, to lead.

'That's everyone, besides Hill and yourself,' I told him.

He agreed.

'Cuppage is unconscious,' I reminded him.

'Mack says he speaks for Cuppage,' he told me.

I asked after his own status. Was he going south, too?

'I have just been there,' he said.

I assembled the group, and addressed the assembly without anger. I told them I could only argue from all I had observed. And that I have always been open to reason. But that I was convinced that at present no hope lay to our south, at least not until the rains returned.

While we were gone they killed the rest of the bullocks and scraped and sewed their hides to carry water for just this eventuality. They will take one cask and leave one. One dray, carrying only Cuppage, the water, and some dried beef and flour. Mander-Jones can almost no longer see from the bites of the flies. Nevertheless, he is leading. He refuses to talk to me at any length. I asked what he wanted done with his specimens and notes and then regretted the meanness of the question.

December 1st

They are gone. The dogs that are left followed them out of camp.

December 2nd

Hill has made a stew of some of the beef. At the last moment Browne tried to arrest the mutineers' departure with a startling display of passion. Now he seems to have withdrawn into himself even more. 'Do you think they have any chance?' I overheard Hill murmur some hours later while serving him his stew. Whatever he answered caused poor Hill to weep once he'd returned to his cooking-fire.

December 5th

A squall has levelled our remaining tents and torn away the canvas covering of our dugout. My papers are gone. What's left of our supplies has been scattered. I found a sextant and two goose quills.

The weather is becoming even more infernal. A gale unrelentingly blows from the N or E. The flies do not relent. How is human foresight to calculate upon such a climate? We are all suffering from piercing pains in the joints. My gums are now hugely swollen. Hill's lower leg muscles are so contracted he cannot stand.

We sit about with the aimlessness of Aborigines, gazing into each other's eyes and preparing for the worst. Only when thinking of my companions do I have regrets at what lies ahead. One of my father's favourite resolutions was always that life was worthless save the good that one might do. 'We're forced to conclude, then, that for him, life was worthless,' Browne remarked, during one of our early father-discussions.

December 11th

We have pains and do not understand what they are. Browne has become unresponsive, immersed in his own unwinding. He has spoken of starfish and sea ferns. I do not know what we will do if he is laid low. He has always been one of those whom life pushed from one place to another. A useful naysayer, the kind Australians call a 'no-hoper'.

December 23rd–24th

Hill is unable to walk. Browne and I have resolved to assay one of the unexplored ravines to our E. He speaks of a great flood there and drowned cattle. Hill looks at him through his tiny spectacles with pity. Hill says he feels no pain while stationary. The skin of his calves and thighs is black and the discoloration is proceeding upwards.

Our horse led us up a draw all night while we dragged along behind it. Daybreak found us in a smallish box-canyon of some sort, sheltered, at least, from the sun. Browne then slept while I explored as best I could. It was an extraordinary place, and evidence of our Inland Sea. There were marine fossils and conglomerate rock which looked like termite mounds. The remains of strange undersea plants and fish-fins were clearly evident in the rock faces. Grotesque shapes, and a great silence. I roused Browne to show him. We were both tearful at the sight. 'The Beadle Sea,' he said to himself, when he came around and saw. 'No, no, the Browne Sea,' I answered, cradling his head, but by then he was again already asleep.

I lay myself beside him, grateful for his presence. He always doubted my judgement but thought my leadership to be worth my blunders. We awoke some hours later to find the horse gone and twilight coming on. More sleep, Browne in a half-conscious state and making small gesticulations. It was as if he had been submerged in a kind of gloaming of the mind, an infant's fatalism.

Near daybreak the moon rose in the E, and the sun followed, warming us both. It was not possible to tell how long my friend had been dead. I eased my arms from around him and stood, and turned round myself, and cried. I squatted beside him. When the sun was full on my head I found a flint and scratched on to the rock face beside where he lay: J.A. BROWNE S.A.E. DEC 25, 1840. I sat with my back to his side for another full day, taking only a little water at sunset. In the blue moonlight the stars seemed to multiply and wheel. I gazed upward, full of grievance and self-justification. I called out that we should be done justice to. The canyon walls gave back their response. In the moonlight they became a luminous cerulean. I heard the slosh and slap of water in a great bay. I knew I had had a dream past the wit of man to say what dream it was. The wind picked up. My ears filled with sound. The blackness of a sandstorm dropped over the canyon rim like a cloak. Its force turned my friend on to his side. Its force turned my face to the rock. I saw strange wraiths. Worm-like, coiling figures. Terrible faces. My eyes clogged with grit. I hoped they would fill with everything they needed. While my throat filled with what poured from the canyon rim. And my heart filled with the rest.

□

WHERE IS THY STING-A-LING-A-LING?

James Lasdun

Forest Lawn Memorial Park

Aneighbour of mine who did tree work for a living was killed up a sixty-foot maple after a branch he was cutting from the crown fell the wrong way, wrapping its anchor rope around his chest and asphyxiating him. He was a young man, the father of two small children, and his funeral, at our town in the Catskills, was crowded with friends and relatives in a state of raw grief. In the slow-moving line outside the funeral home people were sobbing, clutching each other, and exchanging details of the accident in incredulous whispers. The fire department didn't have a tall enough ladder to reach his body. They had to borrow a bucket ladder from a local contractor. He was blue by the time they grappled him down...

I knew he was to be cremated and although this was the first funeral I'd attended in America, I had assumed there would be something like the English-style plain coffin set apart at the end of the chapel, waiting to be trundled off into the furnace. But as we filed in I saw that in fact my neighbour was lying in an ornate casket with an open lid, and that the reason for the slowness of the queue was that we were each expected to go up and bid him a final farewell. Steeling myself (I'd never looked closely at a dead body before), I stepped up to the bier. He had been laid out in a tunic-like collarless shirt; eyes closed, beard trimmed, a turkey feather placed in his folded hands, and a rifle shell at his shoulder. If indeed he had turned blue, he was now a healthy pink, but he looked powerfully unnatural nevertheless: embalmed and made up; utterly unlike himself, but sufficiently recognizable to seem a kind of sinister, waxen impostor. Though I wasn't a close friend, I liked him a great deal and the sight shocked me. It took me months before I could visualize him again as he really was.

I didn't know it at the time, but what I had experienced was a well-documented rite of passage for expatriates in America. Dennis Barlow, the exiled English poet in Evelyn Waugh's novel *The Loved One* (1948), has to arrange a funeral at Whispering Glades Memorial Park after a fellow countryman dies. He too finds himself confronted with the sight of an old friend pumped full of formaldehyde and glycerine: 'the face was entirely horrible; as ageless as a tortoise and as inhuman; a painted and smirking obscene travesty...'

Whispering Glades is modelled on Forest Lawn Memorial Park, in Glendale, Los Angeles. The place, already a tourist attraction in

Waugh's day, complete with its own museum, is celebrating its centenary this year. I visited it at the end of a long train journey from New York, driving through its massive iron gates on a bright morning in June. A gabled Tudor manor (modelled on Compton Wynyates in Warwickshire) stands at the entrance, housing the main offices and showrooms. I had been offered a private tour and I went in to meet my guide, Bob, a dapper, silver-haired employee of twenty-seven years' standing. For some reason I had imagined that our tour would be on foot; that we would stroll musingly among the plots, as I had remembered doing years ago in Père-Lachaise. But this is LA, and as with the living so with the dead: you drive.

The place occupies a 300-acre hill, referred to in the literature as 'Mount' Forest Lawn. We set off up a broad driveway, making our way along vast, sloping lawns with maintenance crews sweeping and mowing, tall trees sparkling in the sun, and little notices prohibiting the laying of artificial flowers. The first thing that strikes you is that there are no gravestones: the smooth green of the grass is striped instead by flat bronze markers running across it like rows of shiny ellipses.

'Those are all graves?' I asked.

Bob nodded. 'Though we prefer to say interment spaces. It's a little nicer...'

Euphemism has always been a stock-in-trade of the funeral industry, but at Forest Lawn it goes beyond mere language to the place itself: this is a *Memorial Park*, not a cemetery and certainly not a graveyard. Its creator was Hubert Eaton (1881–1966), a Missourian from a family of academics and clergymen, who branched out into mining, went broke, moved to California and wound up selling 'pre-need' burial plots in what was then a sleepy country cemetery. He made a go of this and the success appears to have awakened him to the under-exploited potential of a hitherto disorganized industry. His inspiration consisted of two ideas: first, total integration of funeral services, from embalming to casket sales to burial, cremation, flowers and memorialization; and second, a total repackaging of the concept of death. He put forth these ideas in his 'Builder's Creed' of 1917, employing the visionary terms beloved of successful businessmen. The document is almost as interesting a piece of Americana as the place itself:

Where is Thy Sting-a-Ling-a-Ling?

I believe in a happy eternal life. I believe those of us who are left behind should be glad in the certain belief that those gone before, who believed in Him, have entered into that happier life. I believe, most of all, in a Christ that smiles and loves you and me.

I therefore know the cemeteries of today are wrong, because they depict an end not a beginning. They have consequently become unsightly stoneyards full of in-artistic symbols and depressing customs; places that do nothing for humanity save a practical act, and that not well.

I therefore prayerfully resolve on this New Year's Day, 1917, that I shall endeavour to build Forest Lawn as different, as unlike other cemeteries as sunshine is unlike darkness, as eternal life is unlike death. I shall try to build at Forest Lawn a great park, devoid of misshapen monuments and other customary signs of earthly death, but filled with towering trees, sweeping lawns, splashing fountains, singing birds, beautiful statuary, cheerful flowers, noble memorial architecture with interiors full of light and colour, and redolent of the world's best history and romances.

I believe these things educate and uplift a community. Forest Lawn shall become a place where lovers new and old shall love to stroll and watch the sunset's glow, planning for the future or reminiscing of the past.

A place where artists study and sketch; where schoolteachers bring happy children to see the things they read of in books, where little churches invite, triumphant in the knowledge that from their pulpits only words of love can be spoken; where memorialization of loved ones in sculptured marble and pictorial glass shall be encouraged but controlled by acknowledged artists; a place where the sorrowing will be soothed and strengthened because it will be God's garden. A place that shall be protected by an immense Endowment Care Fund, the principal of which can never be expended—only the income therefrom used to care for and perpetuate this Garden of Memory. This is The Builder's Creed.

The creed now stands incised on a mighty tablet in the middle of Forest Lawn, and our first stop was to admire it. Gazing up at it from the courtyard are The Little Pals—a pair of wonder-struck stone urchins and their floppy-eared pet dog. The statuary is a particular point of pride at Forest Lawn. It was assembled largely by Eaton himself, who became an enthusiastic collector after acquiring Edith Parsons's Duck Baby, a sculpture of a little girl in tears, and went on to commission life-size copies of several Michelangelos. After we had joined the little pals for a respectful moment, Bob told me how Eaton—a man who evidently knew what he liked—had hunted through Italy for a statue of Jesus that conformed to his sunny image of the Saviour; 'but you know, James, he couldn't find a single piece portraying Jesus with a smile on his face!'

We drove on up to the Hall of the Crucifixion/Resurrection, an auditorium built to house one of Eaton's larger discoveries: a 200-foot-long painting of the crucifixion, brought to America by its Polish artist, Jan Styka, for the St Louis World's Fair of 1904 and left behind after its exhibitors failed to pay the customs charges. Eaton found it wrapped round a pillar in a derelict theatre and managed to persuade Styka's son to come to America to restore it. It hangs behind a velvet curtain (the largest velvet curtain in the world, Bob whispered as we took our seats) which rises as the lights dim and a recorded voice guides the viewer, with the help of a spotlight, over the massive canvas, identifying the players in the drama in increasingly sonorous tones as it moves towards the climactic event. Not wanting the 'lovers who shall stroll' to be left on a downbeat note, Eaton held a competition for an equally vast *Resurrection* to follow. The winning painting, descending over the *Crucifixion* as the lights darken once more, features a city with a celestial hill above it. After the show, as you go outside to the terrace, you realize that the artist painted his winning entry to bear an uncanny resemblance to Forest Lawn itself, rising over the bungalows of Glendale.

We moved on, passing the colossal figure of Michelangelo's *David*. On my train journey I had read Jessica Mitford's *The American Way of Death*, which mentions this sculpture in its chapter on Forest Lawn, reporting that a fig leaf was placed on it after shocked mourners complained. I had been expecting a moment of snooty amusement at the sight of this prudish addition, but the fig leaf wasn't there, and in its absence I seemed to be experiencing an odd prudish shock of my own. The figure looked almost Dionysian in the otherwise carefully maintained incorporeality of its context. I asked Bob what had happened to the fig leaf. He smiled, saying it had made the statue look 'almost more obscene'. With a chuckle, he added that the figure always broke in the same place when there was an earthquake—just above the weight-bearing knee—as did the five other copies they had at their other sites around LA (Forest Lawn has grown in recent decades, repeating its formula in Covina Hills, Cypress, Hollywood Hills, Long Beach and Cathedral City). The thought of not one but *five* of these astounding copies (done in the same Carrara marble as the original) was disconcerting.

A funeral cortège passed us, black limos gliding to a halt alongside one of the gardens (I think it was the Triumphant Faith Terraces), figures in shades and black suits climbing out and gathering at the emerald verge of the interment space, while a pair of white-gloved military bandsmen stood with their trumpets behind a statue, waiting to play taps, the whole little scene unfolding with the swiftness and frictionless ease that seems the desired note of social events in LA, and which Forest Lawn was clearly efficient at manufacturing.

On we went, to the Great Mausoleum, a sprawling, soaring, eleven-tiered edifice housing the ashes, or 'cremains', of 20,000 dead. It also holds the Court of Honor, where memorials have been erected to the 'Forest Lawn Immortals'—eight eminences chosen by the board for complimentary passes to eternity. The eight include the Mount Rushmore sculptor Gutzon Borglum, the Tin Pan Alley songwriter Carrie Jacobs-Bond, a provost of California State University and Hubert Eaton himself. More Michelangelos surround them, while on the wall just outside Eaton's nephew and successor, John Llewellyn—presumably an immortal-in-waiting—is photographed with Richard Nixon and the Dalai Lama.

A faint numbness had come over me. I fought it, trying hard to rise to the occasion as we moved through the museum with its odd curios that include a paste copy of the Crown jewels and a real Easter Island head, and then on to the stained-glass *Last Supper*, another stupendous work, set in its own special wall with backlighting that simulates daylight dimming to sunset. (The Venetian casino/hotel in

THE MYSTERY

Forest Lawn, Cypress

FOREST LAWN
MEMORIAL PARK

F LIFE

Las Vegas has something similar in its St Mark's Piazza shopping mall, where a whole day dawns and darkens every hour in the immense artificial sky overhead.) As we watched the cycle complete itself, Bob described to me how Eaton, determined to improve on Leonardo's faded original, commissioned the window from the last descendant of a family of stained-glass makers, Rosa Caselli-Moretti. All went well until the firing of the pane depicting the head of Judas. Five times the artist put the glass in the kiln and five times it shattered. Full of foreboding, she telegrammed Eaton to say that she wasn't sure the Almighty wanted her to finish the piece. Eaton thundered back that of course God wanted it finished. She tried once more and lo... another miracle for the books. Aficionados of early corporate branding can read the story, and a great many others with similar moments of agonizing suspense, in the official biography of Eaton, *First Step Up Toward Heaven,* by Adela Rogers St Johns. Better still, they can hear a present-day historian of Forest Lawn relate the same legends in awed tones on the DVD put out for the centenary.

Back in Compton Wynyates we took a look around the showroom where the various burial and cremation packages offered by the cemetery are displayed. For a few thousand dollars you can opt for 'A Simple Goodbye': refrigeration, cremation, flowers, urn, nicheside ceremony and 'memory folders'. For upwards of around $20,000 you can take the 'Elegance Package', with embalming, two days of visitation, leather memorial book, floral tribute, Dove Release, your choice of four caskets (the Alabaster, the President, the Classic Gold, the Monticello), a Bronze Triune Vault to place it in, and so on.

The cost goes up depending on the final location you choose for your loved one. ('This may sound strange,' Bob offered, 'but prices are higher if there's a view.') You don't have to buy a package: individuality is encouraged, and several of the display cases contained suggestions of how to customize, with golf, gardening and baking motifs woven in among the matching leather memory folders and cross-sections of different kinds of casket ('We find people are troubled by the sight of full-length caskets...'). In the subdued light, these glassed-in tableaux looked a little like the dioramas at the Museum of Natural History in New York. An embalmed human or two, swinging a favourite niblick or smiling at a tray of scones, would not have looked out of place. The embalming rooms, as it happened, were directly above us, and I asked if I could see them. 'I'm afraid not,' Bob replied, looking rather shocked. We parted company soon after.

In need of a break, I took a drive around Glendale, a surprisingly seedy neighbourhood containing a large number of retirement homes and medical-supply stores. I ate an oily *relleno* at a Mexican restaurant near a dusty-windowed establishment calling itself the Anti-Ageing Institute. Replenished, if not exactly refreshed, I returned to Forest Lawn to have another look around on my own.

It was hot now, and the place seemed even emptier than it had in the morning. Maintenance crews were picking up dead flowers, otherwise there was almost no one about. I drove along Inspiration Slope, past Tender Care, to the Court of Freedom, where Walt Disney is buried. A little mermaid keeps him company, but the official theme here is America: George Washington statue; mega-mosaic of the signing of the Declaration of Independence. Though it was once segregated, Forest Lawn is now multi-ethnic and non-denominational (most of the newer grave-markers bear Asian names, and Bob had told me proudly that they now do all kinds of ceremonies here: Buddhist, Mariachi, Biker...). Eaton's overt Christianity is presumably no longer a selling point, and with most of the great episodes of American history burdened with troubling associations of one kind or another, 1776 has become, *faute de mieux*, the theme of choice, providing almost all of the uplift at the newer sites. One feels for the proprietors, now that revisionist historians are beginning to get their teeth into even that sacrosanct moment. What would be left, I wondered, for the next generation of Forest Lawn franchises? Marble astronauts was all I could think of.

Next to the court stands the Freedom Mausoleum, yet another vast necropolis. I wandered inside, staring up at the rows of locker-like niches stacked floor to ceiling in the high walls of the Sanctuary of Humility, the Columbarium of Victory, the Corridor of the Patriots. I remembered from Mitford that the tall ceilings of these structures had less to do with solemnizing than money-making (the higher the walls, the more the niches, the greater the profit per square foot of real estate). I tried to recall the formula of spurious logic that Mitford identifies as the basis of the lucrative American funeral industry: the purely invented 'tradition' of embalming (imposed on the public at large after someone made a lot of money doing it with soldiers in the Civil War), from which springs the highly profitable business of selling fancy caskets, which in turn necessitates the purchase of steel or concrete 'vaults' in which to place them so that the ground above doesn't sag... But as sometimes happens when you visit the shrines to the American entrepreneurial spirit, the sheer scale of the place, along with the aura of absolute, intact conviction in its own underlying principles, has a crushing effect on one's pre-emptive cynicism. You feel merely dazed.

Coming out at the Dawn of Tomorrow Wall Crypts, I drifted across the shaved sward of Brotherly Love, one of the more expensive areas, where string music swells night and day from invisible speakers in the laurel hedges. The next gardens along were locked: the Hadean equivalent of a gated enclave. On the door was a bronze plaque which read: ADMITTANCE TO THESE PRIVATE MEMORIAL GARDENS IS RESTRICTED TO THOSE POSSESSING A GOLDEN KEY OF MEMORY, GIVEN TO EACH OWNER AT TIME OF PURCHASE. Lacking a golden key of memory, I got back in my car, looping past the Wee Kirk o' the Heather, then down around Inspiration Slope to Babyland, a heart-shaped lawn presided over by a giant smiling toddler in a bronze diaper. A little further along was Lullabye Land, also heart-shaped, with the Disney castle gleaming in marble at the top.

I could see why Waugh was drawn to the place. Its kitschiness and religiosity make it an irresistible target. But it is so unashamedly what it is that it achieves a kind of immunity to satire, indeed to almost any comment at all.

Waugh himself recognized the ineffectuality of mere disdain as a response to the place. He has his poet-protagonist Barlow succumb to its strange, hypnotic force and fall in love with a young mortuary cosmetician. The twist doesn't add much force to the novel, but it did give me a point of reference for a little Barlowish moment of my own. I was loitering next to the Finding of Moses Pool, trying to figure out the depleted, desolate sensation that the place had left me with, when a black-clad attendant trailing the scent of gardenia materialized before me and asked if she could help. No doubt I'd been spotted on a security camera with my notebook and she had been sent to investigate, but she was strikingly attractive, and I thought of the passage where Barlow's cosmetician comes upon him writing a poem in one of the gardens: 'her eyes widened. "Did you say a poem?"' Lacking a poem of my own, all I could think of to impress my apparition was the joke about the woman who finds a rabbit in her new refrigerator.

'This is a Westinghouse, isn't it?' the rabbit asks.

'Yes.'

'Well, I'm just westing.'

My cross-country train route to Los Angeles had taken me through New Mexico, with a stop in Lamy, not far from Taos and the San Cristobal ranch where D. H. Lawrence lived and where his 'cremains' were brought from France. I'm not usually the pilgrim type, but I had recently written an introduction to a new edition of Lawrence's novella *St Mawr*, which he composed at this ranch, and I was curious to see it.

The place has been preserved by the University of New Mexico. There are a couple of newer buildings, as well as the small chapel that Frieda Lawrence built in her husband's memory, with its homemade-looking phoenix sculpture and window of stained-glass sunflowers; otherwise few signs of change.

Inside the chapel, people had left tiny offerings: a feather, a sprig of juniper berries. Outside, a strong, steady breeze hummed in the treetops. I went down the zigzag path to the adobe-walled ranch house. The great ponderosa pine described in *St Mawr* still stands over the rickety porch, its cones 'open in the sun like wooden roses'. Beyond it a couple of sparrows were building a nest in the bleached skull of an elk nailed to the gate of an overgrown garden.

St Mawr ends with a detailed evocation of the ranch, where Lou Witt and her mother have come, Lou in search of a meaningful life, her mother in search of a meaningful death. Back in Europe, the mystery of death had been reduced, for Mrs Witt, to a larky line in a popular song from the trenches, *O death, where is thy sting-a-ling-a-ling?*, and her salvation seems to depend on her being able to embrace the 'mysterious malevolence' of the wild, primordial landscape surrounding the ranch.

I was thinking of this visit as I took one last drive around Forest Lawn. Among the English churches replicated here is St Giles' in

James Lasdun

Stoke Poges. This was where Thomas Gray wrote his elegy, but Gray's sentiments are unimaginable here. The Builder's Creed has no place for turf heaving 'in many a mouldering heap', let alone 'paths of glory' leading 'but to the grave'.

On the other hand, O *death, where is thy sting-a-ling-a-ling?* would fit very nicely. ☐